AMAZING AUSSIE DOGS

Laura Greaves is a multi-award-winning journalist, author and proud 'crazy dog lady'. She has spent more than twenty years writing for newspapers and magazines in Australia and around the world and is the former editor of *Dogs Life* magazine. Now a freelance writer, Laura has written extensively for countless dog and pet-specific print and web publications. She is the author of the collections *Incredible Dog Journeys*, *Dogs with Jobs*, *The Rescuers*, *Miracle Mutts*, *Extraordinary Old Dogs* and *A Dog's Best Friend*, the children's book *Amazing Dogs with Amazing Jobs*, as well as three romantic comedy novels, *Be My Baby*, *The Ex-Factor* and *Two Weeks 'til Christmas*, all of which feature an extensive supporting cast of cheeky canines.

Also by Laura Greaves

Be My Baby
The Ex-Factor
Two Weeks 'til Christmas
Incredible Dog Journeys
Dogs with Jobs
The Rescuers
Amazing Dogs with Amazing Jobs
Miracle Mutts
Extraordinary Old Dogs
A Dog's Best Friend

AMAZING AUSSIE DOGS

LAURA GREAVES

MICHAEL JOSEPH
an imprint of
PENGUIN BOOKS

MICHAEL JOSEPH

UK | USA | Canada | Ireland | Australia
India | New Zealand | South Africa | China

Michael Joseph is part of the Penguin Random House group of companies,
whose addresses can be found at global.penguinrandomhouse.com.

First published by Michael Joseph, 2022

Cover design by Luke Causby © Penguin Random House Australia Pty Ltd
Front cover photo courtesy Adobe Stock, back cover photo courtesy J Christian
Typeset in Sabon by Midland Typesetters, Australia
Printed and bound in Australia by Griffin Press, an accredited
ISO AS/NZS 14001 Environmental Management Systems printer.

A catalogue record for this
book is available from the
National Library of Australia

ISBN: 978 0 14377 992 6

penguin.com.au

*We at Penguin Random House Australia acknowledge that Aboriginal and Torres
Strait Islander peoples are the Traditional Custodians and the first storytellers of the
lands on which we live and work. We honour Aboriginal and Torres Strait Islander
peoples' continuous connection to Country, waters, skies and communities.
We celebrate Aboriginal and Torres Strait Islander stories, traditions and
living cultures; and we pay our respects to Elders past and present.*

For Ernie and Cilla; Robbie; Missy;
Tex and Delilah; Coco and Ferdinand.

This book is dedicated to all of the amazing
Aussie dogs I've been lucky enough to share my
life with. Every single one of them has helped
to shape me into the person I am today.

Thank you for everything.

Thorns may hurt you, men desert you, sunlight turn to fog;
but you're never friendless ever, if you have a dog.
Douglas Malloch

Contents

Introduction

Growing up, I was fortunate to always have at least one dog. My parents had a pair of West Highland White Terriers called Ernie and Cilla, and when I came along the dogs immediately appointed themselves as my security detail.

We have sweet home movies that show chubby baby me playing on a blanket in the garden while Ernie and Cilla stand guard between me and anyone who might approach. Nobody was getting near me without their express permission, thank you very much.

Nobody taught them to do that. They just instinctively understood that I was the most vulnerable pack member and therefore in need of the most attention and protection.

Amazing.

The next family dog, Robbie, also a 'westie', would pause multiple times during every walk to execute a full 360-degree roll on the grass. Actually, come to think of it, he wouldn't even pause – he would simply somersault mid-stride and then keep walking. We called them 'Robbie's rollovers'.

Who knows why he did that. I imagine he simply found it fun. It was Robbie's way of sneaking a little bit of extra joy into his day. Dogs are experts at that.

Amazing.

Then came Missy. She was the oddest four-legged friend I've ever had, and I found her weirdness completely delightful. Missy hated the mere sight of a camera (which is why I have exactly two photos of her, even though she lived to be nearly fifteen), but not quite as much as she despised the sound of somebody blowing a raspberry. Either of these horrors would send her straight into the darkest corner of my mum's walk-in wardrobe, from where she would have to be physically extracted at dinner time.

What was so upsetting about a camera or a crude noise? I couldn't possibly say. All we knew was that Missy hated both of them with the fire of a thousand suns, and hiding in the wardrobe was, in her mind, the appropriate response.

Amazing.

The first dogs I had in adulthood were Tex and Delilah the Nova Scotia Duck Tolling Retrievers. Tex, as long-time readers of my books will know, had the same approach to medical problems as I have to handbags: collect a lot of them, and make them expensive.

Every time I rushed him to the emergency vet with a new ailment, the specialists would tell me he almost certainly had some catastrophic illness or injury. But then the test results would come back and he wouldn't have the expected thing after all. Or he *would* have it, but it wouldn't do what it was supposed to do.

When he was diagnosed with chronic indolent leukaemia, for example, we were told that it would be at most eighteen months before it would require treatment. In fact, Tex lived another four years without ever receiving treatment for leukaemia, and at one point blood tests showed the condition had disappeared entirely. He was both a medical mystery and a medical marvel.

Amazing.

Delilah, meanwhile, was an empath. I suffer from anxiety and sometimes experience panic attacks, and Delilah somehow always knew to come and sit next to me until I felt better. The feel of her soft fur beneath my fingertips could calm me like nothing else. How did she know that she was exactly what I needed in those moments?

I'll tell you how: she was amazing.

Now I have Coco, a border collie–kelpie mix, and Ferdinand, a flat-coated retriever. Coco can jump 2-metre fences with almost no effort (and did so twice while she was at the local RSPCA shelter, almost scuppering her chances of adoption). Ferdy is a gentle soul with an absurdly deep, loud bark; he has made more than one postman flee in alarm.

They are both amazing, too.

And so is your dog. As the writer WR Purche once said, everyone thinks they have the best dog – and none of them are wrong.

Dogs don't have to do anything in particular to qualify as amazing. They are amazing just by virtue of existing. The 15,000 pictures you have on your phone of your pooch doing not much is proof of that. Dogs are amazing because they love us and protect us and want to please us above almost anything else. And they are very, very cute.

Think about it: 10,000 years ago, a particularly brave wolf decided he was hungry enough to approach a human campsite, looking for snacks. And that single moment of courage led to devoted companions that work for us, protect us, comfort us when we're scared and literally save our lives – just because they like us.

Honestly, it does not get more amazing than that, in my opinion. Dogs are quite simply a gift we do not deserve.

That said, there are many dogs whose amazingness goes above and beyond, and they are the dogs you'll find in this book. These fourteen courageous canines were already amazing to begin with; what they have accomplished makes them extra, ultra, *mega* amazing.

Frankie the German shepherd walked 4000 kilometres to help his owner recover from drug addiction. Bruno, also a German shepherd, was lost in the wilderness for a week but risked everything to get home to the woman whose life depends on him.

Yale the Labrador helped schoolchildren rediscover their love of learning after the COVID-19 pandemic. Buddy the beagle survived eight years as a medical-research test subject and is now fighting for other dogs like him. Kimmy the kelpie sold for a staggering amount at a working dog auction.

See? AH-MAY-ZING.

Even better, they are all Australian. It is often said that this country was built on the sheep's back, but it's fair to say we were built on the dog's back, too. (After all, dogs were the ones rounding up the sheep.) They have been a part of our lives – part of the very fabric of Australian culture – for as long as humans have inhabited this land.

Aussie dogs are, I think, unique among canines. They are among the toughest, boldest and most indefatigable dogs on the planet. They're some of the silliest, too – even our dogs have that Aussie larrikin streak.

So I hope you enjoy the stories in *Amazing Aussie Dogs*. I hope you're moved and inspired and wowed by our homegrown doggy heroes. Because they are truly amazing, each and every one.

And when you've finished reading, I hope you'll look over at your own dog and remember just how amazing they are, too.

Kimmy

The top-dollar dog

What is a dog worth?

It's a question that has both simple and complex answers. The simple answer, of course, is that dogs are invaluable. Their worth can't be calculated with something as prosaic as money. After all, how do you put a price on unconditional love? What would you pay for a lifetime of loyalty, countless nights of cuddles on the sofa, endless days of joy and play? All the cash in the world couldn't even begin to cover it.

The complex answer, however, is that dogs *do* have monetary value. Rightly or wrongly, few of us are able to welcome a dog into our lives without paying either a breeder or an adoption fee. But even then, who decides what's a fair price?

In 2014, a golden-haired Tibetan mastiff puppy reportedly sold for an incredible A$2.8 million at a pet fair in China. Meanwhile, a Sydney-based greyhound rescue group dropped its adoption fee to just $30 per dog in an effort to find homes for as many dogs as possible during the frigid winter of 2022.

Why are some people willing to pay thousands of dollars for a pedigree pooch when a rescue dog that's every bit as deserving of a loving home might set them back just a couple of hundred?

It's a quandary that probably won't ever be resolved to every dog lover's satisfaction. But there *are* some dogs whose value is comparatively easy to determine. That's because they do the same job as a wage-earning human being – except in many cases, they do it better.

Kimmy the kelpie is one of those dogs.

Kimmy's first owner, Kahlee O'Leary, has always had a sharp eye for a dog with potential. Born into a farming family that owns a sheep farm at Elong Elong, near Dubbo in New South Wales, Kahlee has been surrounded by working dogs since day dot.

'I've always been passionate about dogs. If we ever had a litter of puppies on the farm, I'd be trying to have them all on my lap at once. I'd spend hours out in the dog kennels ever since I was little,' she recalls with a laugh.

In her teens, Kahlee's daily trip on the school bus took her past the home of Geoff 'Toby' Lindsay, an internationally renowned working dog trainer and breeder. She would crane her neck to catch a glimpse of Toby in the yard, working his border collies in preparation for competition in the sport of sheepdog trialling.

Kahlee, who was already interested in training working dogs and keen to get started, was in awe of Toby's deft hand with his dogs. She was convinced he was the best person to show her the ropes.

'I bought a ten-dollar kelpie mutt called Ellie from a working dog auction and trained her to sit, stop and stay. I was so excited. Then I asked Mum to take me to see this fella,' she says. 'Toby took one look at my dog and said, "If you get rid of that one, I'll give you one."'

She duly re-sold Ellie at the same auction, sending the little dog off to her new life as a promising working dog. Ellie fetched $50, a solid return on Kahlee's $10 investment and an early indication of her aptitude for identifying and shaping top-quality working dogs.

True to his word, Toby gave Kahlee the choice between two border collies, both of which he had bred. She chose a dog called Judy, then promptly changed her name to Ruby. 'I just didn't think Judy was a very doggy name!' she says.

Kahlee worked closely with Toby, who passed away in 2021, for about five years. She says he taught her everything she knows. He competed in both Australia and New Zealand and was instrumental in developing sheepdog trialling into the competition it is today.

'Toby was amazing. He was a very encouraging person for anyone interested in getting into dogs and livestock.

He never held anything back,' she says. 'I think that back when he was learning, everything was a secret and no one told anybody anything. So whenever he learned anything, he was always happy to share what he knew.'

Kahlee wasn't the only fledgling working dog trainer to benefit from the wisdom of Toby's lifetime of experience.

'Whenever I was there, there was always someone else there that he was helping. He must have taken in a few strays off the street! I think he just put a lot into people coming into the sport,' she explains. 'He was old school and always invited me into the house. He would offer me a cup of tea and a biscuit. He was like another grandfather to me. He was a very cheeky man, too – he had a lot of yarns!'

Toby even competed with Ruby in trials on Kahlee's behalf when she was away working in the mining industry. Because trials take place over several days, it can be difficult for full-time workers to participate.

'It's more of a retired people's sport. When I was first competing, there was me and one other girl in her twenties, a couple of people in their forties, and the rest would have been sixty-plus, right up into their eighties,' she says. 'They struggle to get a lot of younger people coming into the sport.'

(Ruby, incidentally, is now thirteen years old and has retired to Kahlee's brother's country pub where she is 'as fat as a fool and living her best life getting fed by caravaners'.)

With Toby as her mentor, Kahlee's passion for working dogs only deepened – not just training them for competition in dog sports, but breeding and training dogs so she could put her own team together for work in agricultural contracting.

'I've always been in and out of it, but in the last three years I've really tried to get a dog team together again. I've always had between three and seven dogs in my team. My oldest dog now is five, then there's a four-year-old and a three-year-old, a twelve-month-old and a little puppy,' she says.

And as the nature of her work and the requirements for her canine co-workers have changed, Kahlee has also become used to regularly buying and selling dogs. While it may seem a little unusual to city dwellers, who tend to keep a dog for its entire life, it's common for working dogs to have several homes in their lifetime.

'I travel a lot, and I've had to sell a few dogs when I'm travelling. I spent a year living in Canada, so I couldn't take any dogs there. Then I was in mining for four years and not working in agriculture at all – that was hard.'

In November 2019, Kahlee bought an eight-week-old kelpie pup called Kimmy from a breeder in Violet Town, in north-eastern Victoria. Her plan was to train Kimmy up to work and then breed her when she was old enough.

At that point Kahlee's team was a little testosterone-heavy, and she was keen to even things out. 'I had a couple of really nice boys in my team, but I didn't have a female.

I bought her from a breeder that has sold dogs at auctions for over twenty thousand dollars, so having that reputation I thought, *He's obviously got good dogs.*'

Kimmy's price tag was nowhere near that high: Kahlee paid just $800 for her. But it wasn't long before the little pup was showing that she had plenty of potential to become a talented and tireless worker.

'A lot of people will have a specific dog for each task on their property, but Kimmy became a true all-rounder,' says Kahlee. 'She's got experience in different terrains: flat country, hilly country, through creeks. Different environments and different farms. She can go to work tomorrow and you know that she can do whatever you want her to do that day.'

As well as her skill in the paddock, Kimmy has a heart of gold. Some working dogs shy away from affection and have no interest in being pets – they want to work and that's it. Kimmy was definitely *not* that way inclined. 'She's very needy. If you pat her, you can't *stop* patting her. She loves to be in contact with you with her body – she'll lean up against you.'

But farmers and working dog trainers share a sixth sense for that special something in a dog, and even with her work ethic and sweet temperament, Kimmy didn't quite have the X-factor that Kahlee was looking for.

'I'm always trying to find dogs that suit me, and Kimmy was not quite there for me. She was a very nice-natured girl, but she was not calm enough. She was always excited.'

But she knew that Kimmy would be the perfect working dog for somebody else. She already had experience working for a different handler and had knocked his socks off.

'I went travelling around Australia for six months and she went to another farm, where her handler was male. Nobody but me had ever really worked her, so it was really good knowing that a man was able to handle her as well as me,' says Kahlee. 'He loved Kimmy and did not want to give her back. His son told me, "You're going to break his heart. They make googly eyes at each other – it's disgusting!"'

And so Kahlee made the tough decision to sell Kimmy at auction – but not just any auction. She would take her to one of the largest and arguably the most prestigious working-dog auction in Australia: the Australian Kelpie Muster at Casterton in south-west Victoria.

It's not often that an entire breed of dog can be traced back to the very first of its kind, but the origins of the iconic Australian kelpie are as deeply woven into the history of Casterton as its sheep and the meandering Glenelg River.

The first dog to be called a kelpie was born on Warrock Station, just north of Casterton, in 1872. Her parents were two collie-type sheepdogs, descendants of dogs brought to Australia from Britain in the early part of the nineteenth century.

Warrock's owner, Scotsman George Robertson, gave the floppy-eared black-and-tan pup to a stockman called Jack Gleeson in exchange for a horse. Gleeson named his new canine companion Kelpie, after the mythological shapeshifting water spirit of Celtic folklore.

Kelpie later had a litter of her own, and her daughter tied for first place in the prestigious Forbes Sheep Dog Trial in 1879, establishing the breed's working dog credentials. To avoid confusion, the original Kelpie became known as Gleeson's Kelpie, while her offspring was called King's Kelpie, after her breeders, the King brothers. (The Kings went on to establish a breeding partnership with another kelpie breeder, Mr McLeod, and their dogs dominated sheepdog trials for two decades.)

Subsequent litters from both dogs were known as 'Kelpie's pups', and eventually just kelpies.

The traditional owners of Casterton and the surrounding area are the Konongwootong Gundidj Aboriginal people. White settlers arrived in the 1830s and the region's population swelled as first wheat, and then meat, wool and dairy farmers, established a thriving agricultural industry. In the wake of the world wars, the community continued to grow with the arrival of many soldier-settler farmers.

But by the mid-1990s, Casterton – like many rural towns – was in sharp decline. The community came together to consider its future and developed a working party, the Casterton Project 2000, which set an ambitious goal of having 2000 people living in Casterton by the year 2000.

As well as attracting more permanent inhabitants, the working party was determined to put Casterton on the tourist map. They aimed to 'promote the unique benefits and position Casterton as a "must see" township for each and every tourist within the wonderful pastoral area of the Western Districts in Victoria'.

It wasn't long before they settled on an approach for achieving that. One of the town's veterinarians mentioned she had been researching the history of the kelpie and had discovered that the very first one had been born at Warrock Station. The legendary kelpie would be Casterton's unique selling point.

In June 1996, the first Australian Kelpie Muster was held in Casterton across the Queen's Birthday long weekend. The muster includes the one-day Casterton Kelpie Festival, where dog-loving visitors can marvel at the incredible skills of the kelpie. Events include the kelpie triathlon, which comprises the kelpie dash, kelpie hill climb and kelpie high jump. Casterton holds the world record high jump height of 2.951 metres.

Since 1997, the muster has also included the Casterton Working Dog Auction. It was the brainchild of Ian 'Spud' O'Connell, a member of the local Apex Club. O'Connell felt that a working dog auction would be an added draw for both farmers and tourists alike. The first auction netted a total of $6120; in the twenty-five years since, working dog sales at the event have totalled more than $3.2 million.

All of which is to say that, when Kahlee decided to sell Kimmy at Casterton, she knew she was signing up for an event with a pedigree as impeccable as the working dogs that change hands there.

'I had always wanted to come to the kelpie weekend at Casterton. I'd actually lived down there for two years, but because of COVID-19 never got the opportunity to attend before I moved back to Elong,' she says. 'In a way the delay was good, because that allowed me to spend a lot more time fine-tuning Kimmy and making sure she would want to work for other people. I wanted to see what the Casterton auction had to offer as well. I had no idea how Kimmy would sell.'

In the weeks leading up to the June 2022 event, Kahlee entered Kimmy in sheepdog trials in Dubbo, Bathurst and Wellington. Her goal was to help the plucky kelpie get comfortable with the type of environment she would encounter at Casterton: plenty of noise, lots of people and *loads* of dogs.

She handled each new adventure with typical aplomb. In fact, Kimmy was so impressive in the period before the auction that Kahlee almost had second thoughts about selling her. When one of the other dogs in her contracting team became unwell, Kimmy stepped up and excelled.

'She really shone in the last six to eight weeks she was with me. She was working fit, but she almost looked underdone. I thought, *I've got to feed her more!*' People were saying to me, "You must have a great team if you're selling a dog like that."'

But ultimately, much as Kahlee adored her, Kimmy just wasn't the right dog for her. So off to Casterton they went, for Kimmy's perfect family to find her.

For twenty-year-old Ashley Meaburn and her younger brother, Lachlan, sheep farming is well and truly in the blood. The siblings have spent their entire lives on the fourth-generation family farm, Lowick, at Oatlands, 85 kilometres north of Hobart in Tasmania. They work with their father, Damian, and *his* father, Ian, farming 12,000 Merino sheep for their highly sought-after wool and prime lambs.

More recently, the entrepreneurial siblings acquired their own farm and mob of sheep, and have set up an agricultural business called Ashlach Ag.

Sheep and working dogs go hand in hand, and the Meaburn family has never been without at least one trusty sheepdog on hand. 'You have to have working dogs on a farm, so I grew up with them,' says Ashley. 'My father has had kelpies and a couple of border collies. He says he doesn't really have a preference – it's whatever's good and works for him at the time.'

Lately, that's been Huntaways. These big, solid dogs originated in New Zealand and remain the sheepdog breed of choice there. The Meaburn siblings' father, who also works as a Merino sheep classer around Australia, encountered his first Huntaway on a business trip to New Zealand – he was instantly intrigued.

'He just loved their sheepdogs. Ever since then, he wanted one. They're quite big and they've got a really deep bark on them,' Ashley explains.

Their father describes his first Huntaway, Abby, as the best sheepdog he's ever had. When she had puppies in 2019, Ashley took on one of the pups, Winnie, and trained her up to be a reliable worker.

But Abby, who is a very large example of her breed, later developed hip dysplasia – common in Huntaways – and was no longer able to work as hard and fast as she once had. With her hips becoming noticeably worse in 2021, the Meaburns made the difficult decision to retire Abby to life as a much-loved pet and start the search for a new dog to take her place.

With their most-experienced sheepdog suddenly out of action, they didn't have the time to train a puppy from scratch – they wanted a dog that could go to work right away. That's what took them to the Casterton Working Dog Auction.

'The first time we went to Casterton was in 2019, just looking, and we really loved it. It hadn't been on since then due to the pandemic, and when we were looking for a dog it was the first auction on the calendar,' Ashley explains. 'If we hadn't found the right dog there we would have gone to the other auctions.'

In most cases, farmers and agricultural contractors don't just turn up to a working dog auction and buy a pooch they like the look of (well, aside from Kahlee O'Leary's ten-dollar bargain pup, way back when). A top-quality working dog is a big financial investment; the record price paid for a dog at Casterton is $35,200 for Hoover the kelpie, in 2021.

Serious buyers will spend weeks or even months doing their due diligence. About a month before the auction, owners listing a dog for sale at Casterton must upload video footage of the pooch at work. Interested buyers then view the videos and contact the owners for further information, or start bidding if they see a dog they simply must have.

Then, on sale day, each dog completes a short live demonstration for the Casterton crowd. It is also live-streamed for registered bidders watching online from elsewhere in Australia and even overseas.

Kimmy's skill as an all-rounder meant she could handle large mobs of sheep on her own, and work cattle as well. But even knowing what a fantastic working dog Kimmy was, Kahlee says she felt a little awkward at setting what felt like a wildly high reserve price.

'The most I'd sold a dog for prior to that was $4100, and that was a puppy. You tend to kind of undersell them a bit, because you don't want to let down the people that are buying them,' she says humbly. 'You often don't realise that your product is quite good.'

Happily, plenty of other people could see just as clearly as Kahlee that Kimmy is a gem. 'I had maybe four phone calls before the auction and then five interested people on the day that came up to me after Kimmy's demonstration.'

By the time auction day rolled around, Kimmy had met her reserve – and then zoomed right past it. She was already at $13,600 before the auctioneer asked for the first live bid from the 2500-strong crowd.

At Casterton, each dog's owner stands on stage as their pooch is being sold. It was a surreal – and difficult – experience for Kahlee. 'I was really overwhelmed. I was just really happy with how she was on the day. She'd already gone past her reserve, so I knew she was sold. You would think that would have helped, but no. I think that was when I realised, *I've got to let her go*. I wish I could have been as cool and collected as Kimmy was up there.'

She didn't care what price Kimmy ultimately sold for, but she did care who bought her. Privately, Kahlee had her fingers crossed it would be the lovely brother and sister she had spoken to before the event. 'You just want them to go to a good home and be looked after. I'd said to someone before I went up on stage, "I really hope that family buys her!"'

Kahlee wasn't the only one hoping for doting new owners for Kimmy. She had already received a message of support from Grant Little, the owner of another two of her female dogs.

'He sent me photos of them just before I went to Casterton, and they were both on little dog beds in front of the fire. He wrote, *I hope Kimmy goes to a home as good as this one*,' she says.

With their father's guidance, and having studied their videos in earnest, Ashley and Lachlan Meaburn had a shortlist of three dogs they wanted to meet in Casterton. Top of the list was a two-year-old kelpie called Sally, who had already risen to $21,500 in pre-auction bids. Next was Kimmy, and then five-month-old Dusty, who was a 'started' pup, meaning she'd had some training but would need more in order to get her up to peak level. All three dogs were female, which was their preference after having less-than-impressive results with male working dogs.

'You always want to go and see a dog in person. At Casterton they have them all tied up in the barn so you can walk around and see them when they're not working,' Ashley explains. 'You could tell the dogs that were real working dogs. They were like, "Don't pat me – let me do my job and then tie me back up."'

While that might sound like the ideal working dog temperament, Ashley wanted her new companion to be just as comfortable on the couch after a hard day's work as in the paddock. Sally, although lovely and obviously raring to work, didn't strike Ashley as a dog that would enjoy her downtime.

'We've had dogs like that. They're not interested in your affection, they're there to work. That's what Sally was like. If we'd based our decision on the videos alone and hadn't been to see the dogs in person, we probably would have bought Sally,' she says.

But on the day, it was Kimmy who won both her farmer's head and her dog-lover's heart.

'A lot of the dogs were barking, and they would bark *at* you. Kimmy never barked. She was so friendly and well behaved, and her working demonstration was excellent.'

Decision made, the next order of business was to actually buy Kimmy. Ashley and Lachlan wisely left that part of proceedings to their father.

'It's always a bit hard when you go to an auction, because you know anything can happen. Dad buys a lot of rams for people as part of his job, so he's good at auctions. He was the one putting the hand up for us.'

Up on stage, Kahlee admits she was 'a bag of nerves' as bids for Kimmy started rolling in. 'It was quite slow for the first little bit, with the price going up in thousand-dollar increments. When it got to eighteen thousand, twenty thousand, my bottom lip was trembling,' she says. 'Fifteen to twenty thousand is what a good working dog should sell for. Anything above that, people *really* want the dog.'

Several bidders *really* wanted to take Kimmy home with them that day, including the Meaburns. Before Kahlee knew what was happening, the price hit $25,000.

'As it got to twenty-five thousand and then twenty-six

thousand, the auctioneer started going up in $500 increments. It was all a blur to me.'

Out in the crowd, Ashley was feeling the pressure too. The price had exceeded her expectations, but she *knew* Kimmy was the right dog for her, so her father continued to bid on her behalf.

'When it comes down to moments like that, you've just got to do what you've got to do,' Ashley says. 'If you don't want to pay that much, you can just go around the corner to your neighbour and get a pup that you don't know anything about and that probably won't be any good with the sheep. We'd watched Kimmy's video and then saw her live and knew she could do everything we needed, so what more did we want?'

When the hammer finally fell, Kimmy sold to Ashley and Lachlan for a whopping $27,000 – the record price for the 2022 working dog auction. Their original first pick, Sally, achieved the next highest price on the day at $26,000, and Dusty fetched $12,000.

Kahlee was thrilled that Kimmy would be going home with the Meaburns, who had been *her* first pick. And she knew that Kimmy was as perfect for her new family as they were for her. 'I was so relieved when I found out that they were the family that bought her. When they came over after the auction I gave them the biggest cuddle,' she says.

But her elation was tinged with sadness as she faced the prospect of saying goodbye to affectionate and hard-working little Kimmy after two years of working so closely together.

'As soon as I walked off stage I just broke down. I was a mess. It just really opens your eyes to what a good working dog is worth,' she says. 'But you do miss them every day. They're your best mate, really. Kimmy was the fifth dog I've sold at auction, and the two before her were hard to say goodbye to as well. I don't know if I'm getting a bit softer as I get older, but they wriggle their way in. A lot of working dogs do get the family treatment.'

One thing she had no qualms about, however, was Ashley's ability to get the most out of Kimmy.

'You want the dog to work for the next person just as well as they worked for you, and for that person to have the understanding that's needed to work the dog to that level,' Kahlee explains. 'A lot of the time you'll sell a dog and you've almost got to train the person, but I was confident handing Kimmy over to Ashley because I know she can do all of that.'

Kimmy was transported back to Tasmania by friends of the Meaburns, who travelled home separately and were there to greet Kimmy on arrival. Ashley spent a couple of days bonding with her faithful new assistant, and then it was time for Kimmy to go to work.

Just as Ashley had hoped, Kimmy hit the ground running. There was no need for training or getting her used to farm protocol. She simply did exactly what was asked of her from day one.

'Kahlee sent me the same whistle she used for Kimmy in the paddock. I'd never used whistle commands before, so I had to learn how to use that, and then away we went. I blew the whistle and Kimmy did what she was told,' says Ashley. 'When I haven't had any work for her, I've been taking her for rides on the motorbike. If I pass some sheep, she thinks it's a job and I have to say, "Uh-uh." She definitely switches on around sheep, but she has an off switch, too.'

Kimmy has also proved to be the after-hours pet Ashley was hoping for. She has sent Kahlee many heart-warming photos of the little dog snoozing on the couch after a hard day's work.

'When she's not around sheep, she just wants to be with us. She's really sweet. She's a real family dog of a night. She comes in and watches TV and then I put her to bed at seven-thirty and go to bed myself,' she explains. 'She's pretty cool. We're all really happy with her.'

Are they $27,000 worth of happy with Kimmy, though? To the uninitiated, it is a staggering price to pay for a dog, even one that works as hard as Kimmy. Both Kahlee and Ashley frequently field questions from people flabbergasted that a humble kelpie could command such a huge amount of money. The main question is usually, *Why?*

The answer is simple: it's pure economics. A kelpie like Kimmy can do the work of two or even three human farm workers. Each of those employees would typically earn around $50,000 per year, and would usually receive food and board on top of that. Kimmy, meanwhile, costs little to feed, is happy to sleep outdoors, and barring any catastrophes will work tirelessly for five or six years – meaning she only costs around $4500 a year.

In that context, paying $27,000 for Kimmy isn't just a fair price, it's an absolute bargain.

And while achieving such an impressive price for Kimmy doesn't necessarily guarantee that Kahlee's future dogs will sell for top dollar, it's a definite confidence booster. It reinforces that all her years of patient, meticulous training is creating the type of working dogs that people want on their farms.

'Price definitely comes down to the individual dog, but just to know that the money is there for that type of working dog is great,' she says.

Kahlee is already working with another dog she thinks could rival Kimmy in terms of all-round ability. She calls him her 'project' dog. 'He's two years old and I really, really like him. Whether he becomes part of my contracting team or gets sold down the track, I'm not quite sure. It's just exciting to see the new ones coming through – but I can't keep them all!'

So, what is a dog worth? Well, in pure financial terms, Kimmy the kelpie is worth a record-setting $27,000. But, of course, she is worth so much more than that.

The value she had for Kahlee, who recognised her potential, lovingly trained her, and made sure she went to the best possible family, is incalculable.

She's priceless to the Meaburns, too, because Kimmy isn't just an indefatigable team member out in the paddock, she is a gentle presence on the sofa at night. A cuddle-loving sweetheart. A friend to all who meet her.

Amazing from nose to tail.

DJ

The flood survivor

When the rain started on Thursday, Mark O'Toole wasn't particularly worried.

His property is at Bungawalbin, 45 kilometres south-west of Lismore in the Northern Rivers region of New South Wales. It has a creek slicing through it, but that hadn't broken its banks in as long a time as any locals could remember. And while minor flooding sometimes occurs with prolonged heavy rain, it always comes from inland.

Mark's main concern that Thursday, 24 February 2022, was that the country road to the nearby village of Coraki would be inundated, meaning his daughters Eliza, nineteen, and Cheyenne, fourteen, wouldn't be able to get to their weekend jobs.

'Our road gets blocked off pretty easily just from water on the road. I was out at our garlic farm when they rang me on Thursday and said, "Do you think the road's going to go under?"' he recalls. 'I said I thought it might, and they said they'd stay in Lismore so they could get to work at Coraki.'

Sure enough, by Friday morning the road was awash and impassable. Mark couldn't get to his farm, Madison Downs Organic Garlic at McLeans Ridges, just north of Lismore, so he prepared for a day of pottering around at home with his eldest son, Chris, thirty-two. (Single dad Mark also has another son, 19-year-old Texas, who was away working when the rains hit.)

It wasn't just the road that was underwater, though. The swollen creek that traverses his property, an off-shoot of the Richmond River, was rapidly rising. About 20 metres usually separates the waterline from the top of the bank, but that gap was steadily decreasing. Mark was a little alarmed, but thought the worst-case scenario was that he, Chris and their pets might be stuck indoors for a day or two – there was his daughter Eliza's scruffy black-and-white dog DJ, Mr Moustache the cat, and two rats called Angel and Michelangelo.

Mark was actually grateful for the opportunity to get a few household jobs done. The family had only recently moved to the idyllic property, and they were still putting their stamp on their new home.

'I'd bought bedroom suites for the girls and hadn't had a chance to get them built, so since I couldn't get to work, I thought, *I'll stay home and get them all set up,*' he says. 'By Saturday morning, the bedroom suites were floating.'

Mark's home occupies the highest position of three houses on a 140-acre property owned by Lehann Suffolk, who is aged in her seventies. Lehann lives in the second house, and her brother, Murray, resides in the third.

No flood had ever reached Mark's yard before, but the unceasing rain now made it seem like a distinct possibility – and if it got to him it would get to Lehann and Murray's places first. Mark didn't want his neighbours to take any chances; he describes them as 'like family'.

'On Friday I went to see Lehann and said, "Looks like it's going to flood – this rain is not stopping. If the water comes up onto the grass, just ring me and I'll come down and pick you up and bring you up to our house."' Lehann assured him she would call if necessary.

When Mark's phone rang at five-thirty the next morning, though, it wasn't Lehann but Murray on the line.

'He said, "Lehann's down there, floating on her bed." I just went, *Oh my god*. I went straight down to her place,' he says. 'The water had burst through her back door and was going through the house. It was just raging. Lehann was on her bed, which was spinning.'

The swirling, debris-filled water was already up to Mark's chest and he had to grab Lehann and 'drag her by the scruff of the neck' to get her out. At one point the pair lost footing and were swept about 20 metres sideways.

'I thought we were gone, but we got traction again and went up to my place,' he says.

But Mark's house only provided a brief respite. By lunchtime the torrent had reached them, and he had no option but to load Lehann and Chris, who has an intellectual disability, into his tinny on the verandah (a tinny is a small aluminium boat, for any non-boaties). He piled DJ, Mr Moustache, and the two rats into the boat as well, then clambered in himself. It was cramped and uncomfortable, but they were safe and somewhat dry.

All the while, the driving rain continued. By four o'clock on Saturday afternoon, the water was so high that Mark felt it would be dangerous to remain under the verandah. He was stunned by the speed at which the water level had risen, swallowing everything in its path.

'That was very depressing – just watching everything in your life that could float disappear. I had a LandCruiser that's still in the river somewhere. I watched my son's caravan just get lifted up and take off.'

Mark extended the tie rope so that the boat was around the front of the house instead. While they were now fully exposed to the rain and wind, they weren't being quite so relentlessly buffeted by the intense current.

After that, there was nothing left to do but hang on for dear life – and wait. Mark didn't quite know what they were waiting *for*, precisely. It certainly didn't seem like the rain would stop or the floodwaters recede any time soon. He supposed they were waiting for help, but with all phone and internet knocked out he had no way to raise the alarm.

The sun set just before 7.30 p.m., though it had been dark for hours by then thanks to the heavy blanket of black storm clouds. Mark, Chris, Lehann and the pets hunkered down in the boat as best they could. They knew it would be a long and frightening night.

Sunday morning dawned just as grey, grim and wet as the previous three days. What Mark didn't yet know was that Bungawalbin, and the entire Northern Rivers region, was in the midst of the worst recorded flood disaster in its history. In fact, vast swaths of Australia's east coast were underwater, with floods extending from Gympie in south-east Queensland all the way to Sydney, 1100 kilometres south.

By that evening, morale in the boat was understandably low. Neither Mark, Chris or Lehann had eaten anything since late on Friday, and they weren't about to drink the filthy floodwater. DJ, Mr Moustache and the rats were freezing cold and terrified. Lehann was also without her asthma medication. They were all exhausted, drenched and desperate for respite.

About an hour after sunset, Mark thought he heard the *whomp-whomp-whomp* of a helicopter approaching over the roar of the downpour and howling winds.

Sure enough, the blinding searchlights of an Australian Defence Force chopper soon loomed out of the darkness. A lifeline at last.

He watched as the helicopter hovered above the house and its crew deployed a long rescue line, which had weights at the end in an orange plastic bag to control the line in the downdraft. Mark, Chris and Lehann would have been tasked with grabbing the bag in order to be winched into the aircraft, somehow with Mark's pets in tow – but they didn't get the chance.

'They hung there for about five minutes and then took off. It was too dangerous for them with the winds. I thought, *Oh no, they're not going to rescue us.*'

It was a bleak moment.

'It was raining so hard that I had to keep bailing water out of the boat. Lehann was starting to fade. I don't know if she would have lasted another night,' says Mark.

Thankfully, they wouldn't have to find out. Around eleven o'clock on Monday morning, salvation arrived in the shape of the returning ADF rescue helicopter.

But there was more danger to come. As the enormous aircraft bore down on the tiny boat, the incredible force of its downdraft bent the towering surrounding gum trees nearly in half. It also pulled up most of the tin roof of Mark's house. The tinny rocked violently and Mark genuinely feared for his life as he was hit by bits of shrapnel coming off the roof.

'It was this massive, big helicopter, I thought it was going to kill us. I had little bits of tin hitting me in the head. That was the only time I thought I was going to die. I just wanted to tell them to go away!'

Mark helped Chris and Lehann climb onto what remained of the roof to await rescue, then passed Mr Moustache and the rats over to them. He remained in the boat with DJ because he knew his scared dog 'would just freak out' if he were transferred as well.

But as rescue crewman Corporal Geoff Izod was being winched down towards them, Mark suddenly realised another potential catastrophe was imminent. The crewman was aiming to land atop the verandah roof, but Mark knew it would not support the man's weight.

'Every second sheet of the verandah roof was clear plastic, so it was soft. He's gone to disconnect himself from the line and I knew what was going to happen, so I was waving like, *No, no!* He's just gone straight through and into the raging water.'

Mark didn't think twice. He plunged into the turbulent water after stricken Corporal Izod. He managed to grab hold of him, but the weight of the crewman's sodden clothing and equipment meant he was too heavy for Mark to manoeuvre him.

Somehow, both men were able to scramble to safety. Mark's next priority was ensuring Lehann and Chris were winched into the helicopter without further incident. He almost got his wish.

When it was Chris's turn to go up with Corporal Izod, the rescue cable became entangled with the guide rope of a huge aerial on the roof. Mark watched with his heart in his throat as his son dangled precariously 10 metres above the roof while Corporal Izod signalled to pilot Sergeant Damien Collison-Bryant.

Mercifully, Sergeant Collison-Bryant was able to lower Chris and Corporal Izod back onto the roof, disentangle the line and then hoist them up again. Mr Moustache and the rats were also lifted out of harm's way, safely tucked into a bag and hauled up to the chopper.

Then, finally, it was Mark and DJ's turn. Mark decided to wait until Corporal Izod was lowered back down and had disconnected from his safety line before plucking DJ from the tinny. Better to leave the bewildered dog in the relative safe haven of the boat for as long as possible than try to contain him in his arms on the roof as the deafening chopper whipped up a veritable tornado above their heads.

It was a plan that would have worked perfectly if the aircraft's rotor blades hadn't struck a palm tree at that exact moment.

'The helicopter twisted a bit and shredded one of the big palm trees next to the boat. That freaked DJ out. He took off.'

In the blink of an eye, DJ had launched himself out of the boat, vanishing in the wild water.

All thoughts of his own rescue forgotten, Mark leapt into action once again.

'I tried to grab DJ, but ripped a chunk of his fur out instead. He disappeared under the house. It looked like he had gone under the verandah roof, because there was a little gap. I was running along the roof, punching out the clear panels and trying to see if he was in there,' he says.

But there was no sign of poor DJ – and time was not on Mark's side.

'Eventually Corporal Izod says, "Mate, we've got to go." I didn't tell my girls this at the time, but I thought that was it for DJ – I was sure he'd been sucked under.'

Mark had no choice but to join Chris, Lehann and his other pets aboard the helicopter. They were flown to Lismore, exhausted but alive, and in pretty good nick considering their ordeal. Eliza and Cheyenne were there to meet their dad and brother, and Mark had the devastating task of telling his eldest daughter that her canine companion was lost.

The entire rescue had been captured by news cameras and broadcast on live television. Thousands of viewers had watched DJ plunge into the water and feared the worst.

It didn't seem remotely possible to Mark that DJ could have made it out alive – he'd barely survived himself during the couple of unscheduled dips he'd made – but Eliza knows her dog better than anyone. She knew DJ wasn't the type of pooch to give up easily. She wasn't about to give up on him.

Operation Find DJ was about to commence.

*

DJ was named in honour of a man who was dealt a bad hand, and who didn't always make good choices, but who refused to give in.

His name was Dwayne Johnstone, a Wiradjuri man and one of Mark's best friends since childhood.

'I was very close to him, not that I got to see him much,' says Mark. 'He was institutionalised since he was twelve. He spent most of his time either in jail or in foster care and boys homes.'

Dwayne was a tough character, always loyal to his family and friends, but not one for great displays of affection. That changed, however, when he began a new relationship with a woman who had an assistance dog called Lala.

'I'd never seen him show as much affection as he did to Lala. If the dog went out and got thistles in her fur, Dwayne would be the one brushing them out,' Mark says.

He viewed Dwayne's fondness for Lala as a sign that his friend might be ready to lead a more positive life.

'The last time Dwayne got out of prison, his dad and I had a plan in place. We were going to bring him up here to live on the farm and change his cycle of life.'

Tragically, they didn't get the chance. On 15 March 2019, Dwayne was shot and killed by a NSW Corrective Services officer outside Lismore base hospital.

Soon after, Lala gave birth to two puppies, who were named DJ and Dwayne. Devastated by his friend's senseless death, Mark brought ten-week-old DJ home for Eliza.

DJ's breed is a matter of some controversy. He bears an uncanny resemblance to a border collie, and was identified as one in all the news reports about his vanishing act, but Mark is not convinced. 'We think he's a labradoodle–Labrador cross. I've got a friend who breeds border collies and she says DJ is a border collie, but I showed her a picture of Lala, who looks like a poodle.'

Regardless of his genetic makeup, there is no doubt who DJ most resembles in terms of personality.

'We all believe that Dwayne the man is in DJ the dog. Most puppies will just gorge – they'll eat until they're sick. DJ never did that. He'd always look at us like, *Can I eat?* And if you gave him something, even as a puppy, he didn't snatch it off you, he'd take it really gently,' he says. 'DJ also talks to us – he does this little *owowow*.'

And even though he's officially Eliza's dog, DJ isn't stingy about doling out his affection.

'Some dogs are just a one-person dog, but DJ gives us all love,' Mark says.

Mark has had a lot of dogs throughout his life, and he's raised his kids to be dog lovers too.

'I've had dogs ever since I was a kid. Before we moved to Bungawalbin I had a dog and each of my four kids had their own dog. We've always had four or five dogs.'

Sadly, the family hasn't always had good luck with their pets. One of Cheyenne's dogs succumbed to a deadly paralysis tick, while another was callously shot by a neighbour who erroneously believed the dog had attacked his sheep.

But as almost any serial dog owner will attest, while the loss of any four-legged friend is heartbreaking, the joy dogs provide makes the grief worth it – and so we love them again and again.

It was that love for DJ that drove Eliza to launch a full-scale search for him in the days after her father, brother and neighbour were plucked from their rooftop, even when the chances her dog had survived seemed slim at best.

For two days after he disappeared, Eliza posted to every community page and missing pets group she could find on every social media platform she could think of. She pleaded for anybody who might have spotted a black-and-white dog anywhere near Bungawalbin to get in touch.

Of course she hoped against hope that DJ was alive, but even if he wasn't, she wanted to know what had become of him.

No sightings were reported, but a man called Dave Oneeglio did get in touch. Sydney-based Dave was one of an army of volunteers who descended on the Northern Rivers in the immediate aftermath of the floods simply because they wanted to help communities get back on their feet.

'Eliza posted all over Facebook: *Have you seen DJ?* Dave saw the posts, rang us up and said, "We're going to come and find DJ,"' says Mark, who admits he was sceptical. 'Then my daughter heard that someone, a neighbour, had spotted a black-and-white dog out that way.'

The area was still impassable. Houses were underwater; barely any land was even visible. Going in by road was simply not an option, but searching for DJ by boat came with its own set of complications. Mark didn't know how to get from the Richmond River to the stretch of the creek that bisected his property, because he had never had to do it before. And even if they could find a way in, with the waterways full of debris ranging from cars to entire buildings, it was a seriously risky undertaking.

But with help from Dave and two young tradies from Byron Bay, who were also volunteering their time and skills, they plotted a possible route and set out with a jet ski and a boat.

'I went on the back of the jet ski with Dave. The only way we spotted the entrance to the creek was because of the tops of the trees. There was no land,' says Mark. 'But when we got up to our place there was a little bit of land that was up out of the water. I'm thinking, *Oh my god*.'

He got off the jetski and searched his place in chest-deep water, but found no sign of DJ. There was no sign of anything, really: his house was still standing but had been all but destroyed by the flood. Down at Lehann's house, only the kitchen remained; everything else had been washed away. And yet the sight of that small patch of earth filled Mark with hope.

There was also the fact that DJ *loves* water, and is a strong swimmer. 'I get up about 5.45 a.m. and let him out and he'll come back about 6 a.m. wringing wet because he's been in the creek or the dam. He loves swimming.'

Suddenly it didn't seem beyond the realms of possibility that DJ had found his way out of the water. Had he found his own sliver of ground on which to take shelter? Was he out there somewhere, just waiting to be found?

All around them, the signs pointed to a tremendous loss of animal life. Mark estimates he saw at least eighty dead cows and horses as he made his way back to his home. He had put his own chooks up on his roof and on return found most of them dead.

But there were also hopeful signs, as Mark noticed several bush hens alive and apparently unperturbed by the events of the past few days. With renewed enthusiasm, he jumped back on the jet ski and ploughed on. He yelled out for DJ for at least thirty minutes – to no avail.

That was when he heard it.

From what sounded like miles away, so faint it could have easily been missed, came a howl.

Mark drove the jet ski a further 500 metres or so. Just days earlier the area had been bushland, now it was a vast inland sea. He didn't hear the howl again, and was beginning to think he had imagined it, when a strange feeling came over him.

'I was just on the verge of giving up when I got this

feeling to turn to my right. Off in the distance I saw this black-and-white dog stuck on top of a pile of rubble.'

Even as he turned the jet ski and sped towards the dog, he wouldn't let himself believe it could really be DJ. Mark's neighbours from an adjoining property also had a black-and-white dog – this was probably their pooch, not his.

'But as I got closer I thought, *Oh my god*,' he says. 'DJ and the neighbours' dog look identical, so it was not until I got really close that I realised it was actually him.'

Three days and nights after he'd last seen his terrified dog, when she'd been whisked away by angry flood-waters, here was DJ. He was bedraggled and subdued, but very much alive. On closer inspection his little island turned out to be the mangled remains of a machinery shed.

Just as Mark could hardly believe he was looking at DJ until he had absolute proof, it also seemed to take a few moments for DJ to accept that his human had come back for him.

'He wasn't in his right mind, so he wasn't doing what he'd do when I come home from work, for example. He eventually realised it was me and got all excited, but at the same time he was giving me attitude, like, *You're late*.'

DJ's survival was nothing short of incredible. Mark found him half a kilometre from where he'd entered the water. How on earth did he make it?

'Caravans were getting washed past, and he'd gone into that. Where we found him had been eight metres underwater two days before. I think he's held on to a tree branch or something until the water's gone done, and that pile of metal was the next thing that was out of the water,' he says.

Incredibly, DJ wasn't the only animal that Mark, Dave and their fellow volunteers found on their rescue mission that day. They returned to Lismore with ten other dogs and six cats.

When Mark found Eliza and Cheyenne, they were covered in mud because they had been helping to clean up other people's houses. The look on their faces when they saw DJ, says Mark, 'was gold'.

Even better, DJ somehow emerged from his ordeal with no physical injuries. Emotional scars are another matter, though.

'We had him all checked by the vet and he's physically okay, but he's traumatised. He just seems different,' Mark says. 'Normally when I call him he comes, but a few times since the floods I've got close to him and he's run off. He's just doing things a bit differently, which is fully understandable.'

He did enjoy the fame and adulation that came with his remarkable rescue, however. DJ's heroic survival story made headlines around Australia and was also picked up by international news outlets. Celebrity vet Dr Katrina Warren even sent him a new bed and a package of other goodies.

'I had a full day of interviews with all the stations,' says Mark. 'He loves posing for photos.'

DJ was the good news story the Northern Rivers desperately needed. The area was completely devastated by the flood. In Lismore alone, 3000 homes were affected by the disaster. The floods claimed twenty-two lives, including four Lismore residents.

Then, only a month later, on 30 March, the Lismore area was ravaged by another major flood event when the Wilsons River burst through a levee. The second flood forced hundreds of residents to again flee their homes, and more than sixty people had to be rescued from the rising water.

By June, some 1300 families were still not able to return to their homes. Many were still living with friends, staying in short-term emergency accommodation or even living in their cars. In the aftermath of the disaster, federal and state governments were roundly criticised for their failure to help flood victims. Little emergency relief funding was made available in the days and weeks after the catastrophes.

Private companies donated generators, while people around Australia donated millions to flood appeals. Even Hollywood got involved: *Thor* star and Byron Bay resident Chris Hemsworth funded two helicopters for two weeks.

Northern Rivers residents felt abandoned by the agencies and organisations they had expected to come to their aid. Instead, it was the community members themselves who rallied to repair their towns.

When the water eventually subsided, Mark and his family had no home to return to. His garlic farm had been inundated and he had lost much of his crop. So he did the only thing he could think of doing: he helped others.

In partnership with Rotary, he became a driving force behind the Northern Rivers Community Housing Program, an initiative that provides prefabricated modular homes to families who were rendered homeless by the floods.

For more than six weeks after the floods, he spent twelve hours a day on boats, ferrying people and supplies around the district – all while bunking in a house with eighteen others.

In his final week out on the boats, Mark's vessel hit submerged debris and he was flung into the water. He sustained a concussion, broken ribs and damage to his liver.

Within days of being released from hospital, he suffered a crushed hand and almost severed three fingers while working on his own property. That injury required another lengthy hospital stay.

It has been a long, hard slog, and there's still so far to go. But through it all, Mark's family has been by his side, including its most tenacious four-legged member, DJ.

'At the beginning, before we found DJ, it was the miracle that might happen – then it became the proof that miracles do happen,' he says.

Mark counts himself as one of the lucky ones, all things considered. After all, he has a constant tail-wagging reminder that even in the darkest of times, wonderful things can happen.

And those wonderful things often come in the shape of a dog.

Sally

The senior sweetheart

For every dog lover, there is a dog that started it all. They might have shared their life with a dozen different canines, and will have loved each of them fiercely, but there is always one that stands out – one that transformed them from an everyday pet owner to someone whose life is incomplete without at least one dog in it. It's the dog they connected with on a deeper, almost magical level; the dog that changed them in some profound and lasting way. Some call this special four-legged friend their heart dog or even their soul dog.

Karen Goullet called hers Sally.

Sally almost certainly wasn't her original name. Nobody knows what the sweet Staffordshire bull terrier was called by her former owners, because in 2006 they left her tied to a fence outside a council pound at Clontarf, north of Brisbane, with nothing. Not a bed or a toy.

Nothing to eat or drink. No protection from the elements. And certainly no information about her identity or background.

She was at least fifteen years old. For reasons known only to them (and really, there is no reason that could justify it), her owners simply tied her up and walked away.

It was shelter staff who named her Sally. Then they rang Karen.

'I was at work when they rang and said, "Can you pop down and have a look?" I went down after work and she was sitting in the corner of this cage, facing the back. It was quite dark and I really couldn't see her,' Karen says.

Sally was so scared and confused that she wouldn't even look at her. The petrified pup pushed herself as far into the corner of her crate as she could, perhaps trying to make herself invisible. The pitiful sight broke Karen's heart.

'I opened the cage and they said, "Just be careful, she's a bit snappy." I made my way towards her and took her face in my hands and said, "Hello, old girl. You're coming home." She melted into my arms and I just knew I had to love and care for her.'

That day wasn't the first time the shelter had called Karen and asked her to take a dog into foster care. It probably wasn't even the tenth time. Karen and her husband, Jamie, had already fostered countless dogs from this particular shelter and through a local rescue group, Peninsula Animal Aid.

She has always been a dog person. Some people just have that particular kind of love built into them, Karen says. And as soon as her four children were old enough, she signed up to become a foster carer.

'I've just always loved dogs. I saw the issues they face and wanted to help. I knew that if I fostered a dog, then the rescues and shelters had space to take another one in,' she explains.

But from the moment they met, Karen knew Sally was different. She had already been struggling with what many foster carers agree is the toughest part of the arrangement: letting the dogs go. 'As much as we loved fostering dogs, we always had to say goodbye to them because somebody would adopt them. It was playing on my heartstrings. I wanted to keep them all.'

She already knew through her involvement in the rescue world that shelters were full of senior dogs. It seemed that no matter how many years of loyalty and love a dog had devoted to their family, none was immune to being discarded in old age. Some were working dogs that could no longer work. Others were pets whose health was failing, leading to vet bills their owners were unable or unwilling to pay. Still others were replaced by younger dogs that were more active, more 'fun'.

And then there were those like Sally – dumped with no explanation at all.

The senior dogs Karen had seen in shelters were the lucky ones. They had actually made it into rescue and had the possibility of a new life. Many rural pounds weren't even making old dogs available to rescue groups – Karen says they were usually euthanised immediately, and rarely humanely.

She was no longer willing to stand by and let that happen. When Sally came into her life, Karen felt her purpose suddenly become crystal clear.

'Jamie and I sat down one day and he said, "What do you want to do?" and I said, "I want to adopt old dogs." Within two months we had five old dogs, and within six months we had ten.'

And Sally was there to show all the new family members how things worked, just as *she* had been shown by the other foster dogs when she arrived.

'Even though she was really old, Sally was a little bit snappy and a little bit food aggressive, because she didn't know what was going on. She just needed love and affection and time,' says Karen. 'I'm taking too much credit – the rest of the dogs showed her the way. The pack shows them how everything works. She learned very quickly and we never had to separate her, even though she was cranky.'

Occasional bad moods aside, Sally was in remarkably good condition for her age. She was big for a Staffy, with a big, boofy head and a beautifully frosted face. Nobody knew exactly how old she was, of course, but her vet estimated she was around fifteen based on the condition of her teeth.

The vet also cautioned Karen that Sally likely wouldn't be with her for very long.

'He said she was extremely old and wouldn't have much time left. He didn't want me to have high hopes,' she recalls. 'He said, "You know she's going to be a palliative case." I didn't know very much about that at that stage.'

Palliative care helps dogs to live as fully and comfortably as possible with a life-limiting illness that cannot be cured. As soon as she understood what it meant to care for a dog at the end of its life, Karen knew she had to open her home to these dogs, too. 'We put it out there to our rescue contacts that we would help the palliative dogs and they would die here – surrounded by love – instead of in a shelter.'

For her part, though, Sally continually defied the vet's prognosis. She wasn't sick, just old – and that didn't stop her enjoying life with Karen and Jamie to the full.

'When we would take her to the vet for a check-up he was always surprised that she was still alive!'

Sally did have arthritis, so Karen figured out a neat solution that would still allow her to go on her beloved daily walks.

'She loved her walks, but her legs were sore and she was on arthritis medication, so in the end I used to pull her around in a cart. We called her Mustang Sally,' she says. 'It was back in the time when nobody really did that, so people used to laugh at us. We'd be walking her up and down the street in the cart and people would stop and take photos. Sally didn't care – she was just enjoying herself. Everyone knew her and would stop and say hi to her in her cart.'

Eventually, however, time caught up with Sally. In November 2008, she suddenly slowed down and stopped eating. Karen and Jamie rushed her to the vet, but nothing more could be done. It was Sally's time.

Karen was so devastated by Sally's passing that she took a week off work to grieve. And she wasn't the only one who mourned the elderly Staffy.

'Sally really affected people. When she died, lots of people were just so sad. There were people we barely knew genuinely crying because she had passed away,' she says. 'We had two years with her and they were two great years. She hung in there, she really did. I still think of her every day.'

It would be hard not to think of Sally when the evidence of her legacy is everywhere. Her arrival in Karen and Jamie's life had sparked a renewed sense of purpose in them both, and her departure only strengthened it.

'Sally really opened my eyes to the plight of senior dogs. If I hadn't taken her she would have died in that cage. I couldn't live with myself knowing that happens to old dogs every day,' she says. 'When you're younger it's all about me, me, me. Even though we were fostering dogs, we were still spending money left, right and centre on things we just didn't need. Sally taught us that things aren't important – but *she* was. That was a huge lesson. It was like a bolt of lightning, and off we went.'

From one special senior dog to ten within six months, there was no turning back.

When they adopted Sally, Karen and Jamie were renting a property at Redcliffe, a seaside suburb north of Brisbane. Once they decided to become a sanctuary for senior dogs, however, they knew they needed a new place to live. They eventually found their dream home a little further north, in the semi-rural suburb of Morayfield.

Karen admits their senior pack was a top priority when they were house hunting. 'After Sally, we knew we had to save harder to get the property we needed for the seniors. We're on two acres, and we bought this place because of how great it's set up for the dogs,' she says. 'The minute I saw it I said to Jamie, "This is it." We've got pet sheep and goats, which the dogs love. It keeps them busy running around trying to catch them, which they can't. They seem to tell me – in the way dogs do – that they love it here, and they love their lives very much.'

It was fortunate they had all that space, because the old dogs kept coming. In the sixteen years since they adopted Sally, the Goullets have taken in somewhere between fifty and seventy senior and palliative care dogs.

Karen tries to have no more than ten seniors at once, but it rarely works out that way.

'At our maximum we've had fifteen or sixteen. The dogs come to us from different places. It's mostly word of mouth now, but Peninsula Animal Aid still ring me, and there's a few other rescues that we work with,' she says. 'And people still turn up at our door, contact us through Facebook or get our number from somebody.'

Across Brisbane, residents can only have two pet dogs per household. If they want more than that, they have to apply to their local council for permits. With up to sixteen dogs at any given time, that's a *lot* of paperwork for Karen. Fortunately, she says, her council has been very support-ive. Council representatives even sought Karen and Jamie's input when making changes to companion animal by-laws, and Karen feels the new rules are 'a lot fairer and more compassionate' towards pet owners as a result.

The council also nominated Karen and Jamie for its Citizen of the Year Award in 2018.

The COVID-19 pandemic, the skyrocketing cost of living, and the 2022 floods in Queensland have seen the couple inundated with more requests to take in senior dogs than ever before.

Among the most heart-rending owner surrenders she's ever taken in were Timmy and Ruby, a Maremma mix and a red cattle dog. Their owner had a terminal illness, and she was desperate to know her dogs would be loved and cared for after she died.

'She wanted to see the home they would be in, so she contacted us and brought them over. I said, "If you don't think we're the right fit, we understand." She said, "Well, you're the only fit, nobody else will take them."'

Timmy and Ruby settled in well, and their former owner was able to visit them twice before she passed away five months later. On the night she died, the dogs were unusually unsettled. 'Timmy and Ruby were barking and barking, and they never barked at night. I got up and they were all sooky and whining.' She believes they knew their doting former owner had gone.

Karen and Jamie attended her funeral, and were touched beyond measure to discover the woman had written her own eulogy and had included in it a thank you to the couple for caring for her dogs, telling mourners that knowing they were with Karen and Jamie eased her pain.

Karen struggles to turn anyone away, but she is realistic about Jamie's and her capacity to provide quality care – if they bite off more than they can chew, it's the dogs that miss out. At the same time, she sometimes worries that she is already stretched too thin for the dogs in her care.

'When there's one of me and fifteen or sixteen dogs, I have to look at whether they're getting the best care. In saying that, they're in a home with two humans who love them. I spend all day with them, and my whole focus is on them,' she says. 'I often say to Jamie, "Do you think we're giving them the best? There's only two of us and so many of them." He always laughs at me and says, "If I was a dog, I'd want to be here."'

And that's the thing: once an old dog finds its way to Karen and Jamie, it's a permanent part of the family. Not one of the dogs they've taken in since Sally has gone on to be adopted by somebody else. Each and every one has lived the rest of their life with the Goullets.

'They always stay here. That was one of the reasons we set up the sanctuary – they were never going to be adopted. They were always going to be here with our family.'

Sometimes people do say that they would be willing to adopt one of Karen's seniors, which she admits she finds a little frustrating; the huge number of old dogs in pounds and shelters shows that many people talk the talk but aren't prepared to walk the walk.

'I sometimes wonder if each dog would be better off in a house with just one other, but the fact is that nobody else wanted them. We share them on Facebook and people say, "Oh, I would have taken that dog" – but nobody did.'

Karen and Jamie have named their two-acre haven the Sanctuary for Senior Dogs Brisbane (SSDB). Karen has a Facebook page on which she shares pictures and stories, but she emphasises that she's not running a rescue group. She's just someone with a lot of old dogs.

Not only are her dogs not available for adoption, but Karen and Jamie's refuge is entirely self-funded. They neither ask for nor accept monetary donations, although they have occasionally taken pre-loved dog beds and surplus food from caring people whose own dogs have passed away.

Everything their dogs need, from food to veterinary care, is paid for from their own pockets. Jamie works full-time as a mechanic, while Karen also worked full-time in contract management until injuries sustained in a car accident forced her into early retirement.

Or, rather, she swapped paid employment for a new full-time job as an unpaid carer for her beloved dogs.

Understandably, she fields a lot of questions about the costs associated with looking after ten or more senior dogs. Most people assume it's a wildly expensive under-taking, but Karen says that's not the case.

'People say to us all the time: "You must spend all your money on vet bills." But we don't. It's a huge misconception. If you're on top of everything, it's fine. Once we have them on good food and routine vet care, they rarely go to the vet unless something goes wrong,' she explains. 'We put money into a vet account and it rarely runs dry. We don't even like to talk about money, because every cent is worth it. We don't regret one dollar. It's not about us, it's about them.'

Some of the dogs do incur more veterinary expenses than others, but that just makes their transformation after receiving treatment all the more remarkable.

One of those dogs was Josie the Cairn terrier.

When Josie arrived at SSDB in 2020, she had almost no hair and her skin was covered in bleeding sores;

Karen couldn't actually determine her breed until much later. She was also blind and deaf, and she had been abused.

Karen took Josie to the vet, where tests pinpointed the cause of her appalling condition: she was diabetic. Once she started receiving twice-daily insulin injections – one of the most expensive canine medications – Josie's skin quickly cleared up and her beautiful fur grew back.

Despite all her challenges, Josie was a loving old lady with a fighting spirit. She passed away in July 2022, at the age of fifteen, having been loved by Karen and Jamie for two wonderful years.

'She had been terribly mistreated, but she still trusted us and still loved us. She was never afraid of us. She had the best nose in Brisbane and could find her way around the house. She sensed that she was in a good place and she just thrived.'

In fact, none of the senior dogs that Karen has adopted have ever exhibited fear of her, no matter what they have been through in the past.

'I think dogs can sense the good in people. They are the only creatures I've ever seen that can be terribly mistreated but will still give a human that chance, that opportunity, that love. It's an incredible thing to see,' she says. 'We've never had a dog that's been frightened of us or has run and hid behind the couch. They all just trust and reach out for that love. It's as if they think, *Okay, I think he's good and she's good, and I'm going to go with that.*'

That also seemed to be the thinking of Andy the shih tzu when he came to SSDB from the pound five years ago. His black coat was a big, matted mess. The vet that checked him over couldn't say for certain whether Andy had been dumped and was roaming for a long period of time or if he had been abused.

One thing was certain, however: Andy would bite anyone who came near him. None of the shelter staff could approach him. So they called Karen.

Karen agreed to meet Andy, but privately she wasn't sure she would be able to help him either. When she arrived, the staff member who brought Andy to Karen's car was wearing thick welding gloves.

'I had a conversation with Andy all the way home: "Now, Andy, you're coming home and I'm your mum. You're going to love our place. Please don't bite me when I get you out of the car,"' she recalls. 'Sure enough, he didn't bite me. He just knew he was home. He didn't want to be scared and aggressive all the time. He wanted to be happy and loved.'

Karen believes wholeheartedly that the dogs transform when they come to SSDB because they want to stay. They get the care they need, so they feel physically better, but they also try to be on their best behaviour so that they won't have to leave. (Karen is at pains to add that Andy can still be naughty in other ways, but he takes himself off to her walk-in wardrobe for a self-imposed timeout when he misbehaves.)

The dogs don't know, of course, that they'll *never* have to leave. Their experience has taught them that they are disposable, that it could all be taken away at a moment's notice. For Karen, that's one of the hardest things about rescuing senior dogs: the bewilderment they experience when they first arrive at the sanctuary. For many of the dogs, their sense of loss is palpable.

'They come here, and as much as they love being here, we can still see that they're not sure what's going on. Their whole world has turned upside down, and even though we're all set up for them, they wonder why. Making them feel safe and loved is the priority, but sometimes you see it in their eyes and it's just heartbreaking,' she says.

'They all settle in eventually. They understand that this is for real and we're here for them. I love seeing the turnaround. It's just magical when they start running and smiling. We know that we're changing them, because they're so lost when they lose their family or their home.'

She has seen dogs hang on to life for longer than perhaps they should have purely because they don't want to leave the place where they were loved the most.

'One of our girls that recently passed, Riley, had bone cancer. When she was first diagnosed, the vet gave her four weeks – she lived another eleven months. I know it was because she didn't want to leave us. I know it.'

As each new dog does accept that they are home for good, it's hard to imagine the pack ever being without those particular four paws in it. How could SSDB be complete, for example, without Echo, an enormous Labrador who Karen describes as being 'older than Methuselah' and having 'the biggest bark you've ever heard'?

'They called him Echo at the shelter and we kept it, because when he barks you can hear it everywhere,' she says.

And there's Norman, a big Staffy, just like Sally. He's the dog who chose his own name.

'He had some strange name, but I didn't really like it and it wasn't something he'd been raised with, it was just something the shelter named him. So I said, "I think you are a Norman," and he'd picked it up within a day.'

Then there are the deaf dogs. There are several of them and they have all learned hand signals, though Karen still talks to them – much to Jamie's amusement.

There are some blind dogs, too, whose bravery and persistence in navigating their new home never fails to bring a tear to Karen's eye. She keeps the house as stream-lined and uncluttered as possible to make it easier for these special seniors, but admits it can be hard to stand back and let them figure it out. 'The blind ones absolutely amaze me. When you see a blind dog work out a house and a property and become confident to walk around, to me that's absolutely amazing. The courage and the strength of that dog. We don't have that trust, as humans. It's very unique, but dogs have it.'

Caring for old dogs and palliative care cases means that loss is inevitable for Karen and Jamie. They are philosophical about having to say goodbye to members of their senior canine family – but they grieve every pack member, no matter how long the departed dog was with them.

They have a special end-of-life ritual for every dog in their care that crosses the Rainbow Bridge – that wonderful gateway to doggy heaven. The vet always comes to the house, because Karen is adamant that no dog should go to sleep for the final time scared and confused in a sterile vet clinic.

Karen and Jamie curl up on their bed with the dog, which passes away safe and loved in their arms. They always try to keep their own emotions in check so as not to cause the dog any distress.

Afterwards, small dogs are laid to rest in a purpose-built cemetery on the property, while the larger breeds are cremated and their ashes returned home.

And that's when the grieving process begins. 'It never gets any easier. We had a dog in palliative care that was only here for three weeks and I grieved for that dog as much as I would grieve for one that had been here five years.'

What makes it easier is focusing on the quality of each dog's life instead of the quantity. That, and taking in another old dog in their honour.

'We don't concern ourselves with the length of their lives. We don't think, *We're not going to get very long with them,* or *this one's going to go soon.* It never crosses our minds,' says Karen. 'Jamie will often say, "Okay, they might not have been here for very long, but they were very loved." We just take in a new senior and make sure they know they're loved, that they're going to be looked after.'

Besides, no dog whose life ends at the sanctuary ever stays away for long. Karen says she and Jamie receive 'little visits' from their dear departed dogs, including Sally, who still pops in from time to time.

'About a week after Riley passed away, I was reading a book out on the deck when I felt a nose tapping at my leg. That was what Riley used to do. I looked down to see which big dog it was and there was no dog there. I think it was Riley saying, *I'm okay – are you okay?* Jamie never used to believe me when I would say, "Such-and-such visited me today." He thought I was crazy – until it happened to him one day.'

Interestingly for Karen, it has been sharing the sad moments with Jamie that has made her appreciate just how invested he is in their mission to rescue old dogs. He has always been supportive, but when Sally first inspired Karen to devote her energy to saving seniors, she worried at times that her husband was simply being swept along by her momentum.

She knows now that he is fully with her every step of the way.

'Jamie had dogs growing up, but he wasn't as big a dog lover as I was. When we first started this, he was just doing it for me. But then he really got into what we were doing and his passion became just as big as mine,' she says. 'It has really turned his whole world around, and he's a different man because of it. You should see him when a dog passes away in his arms. He was always the strong one and I was the one falling to pieces, but now he's right there with me. "Tough Jamie" wouldn't have been like that in the past.'

Of course, both Jamie and Karen have been irrevocably changed by the senior dogs they have saved – by Sally and every single dog that came after her. The couple has no plans to ever stop saving old dogs, but should a time come when they're no longer able to continue, they hope one of their adult children will carry on their work.

'Our kids all love old dogs, which is wonderful. I worried sometimes that they missed out on a bit from me and Jamie because we were focusing on the dogs. They could have resented the dogs, but they never did,' says Karen. 'They've loved them all.'

It would be easy to ask, *Why wouldn't they?* How could anybody look at the soft grey muzzle of an old dog and not see a lifetime of loyalty and unconditional love? How could anybody deny a senior canine a soft bed, a full belly and all the cuddles they can handle?

But the hard truth is that many people *don't* share the Goullet family's love of senior dogs. They don't see what Karen and Jamie see. If they did, shelters would not be full of golden oldies, and there would be no need for the couple to do what they've done for the past sixteen years.

It's such a shame so many people feel that way, because old dogs are amazing. They are not without their challenges, but those are far outweighed by the rewards.

'We love all the dogs and accept them as they are. We've taken really difficult, hard cases, but love is a powerful thing, it really is,' Karen says. 'We'll take a dog like Andy, a dog that people have said should be euthanised, and he turns out to be just beautiful. We've seen some truly miraculous things happen.'

Sally would be so proud.

Basil

The life-saving Rottweiler

Every decade or so has a 'bad breed' of choice. These are the dogs that find themselves the targets of damning media reports about their so-called vicious temperament. They're branded as dangerous, a threat to public safety, and some are subjected to restrictive state or local government legislation. If popular opinion is to be believed, to choose one as a family pet is to bring a ticking timebomb into your home.

For most of the twenty-first century, pit bulls have unfairly copped most of the flak, despite the fact that just 100 years ago they were known as 'nanny dogs' thanks to their well-documented affinity for children. In the nineties, the Doberman was inexplicably in the crosshairs, and the German shepherd endured an unwarranted period of infamy too.

But back in the eighties, the breed most often accused of bad behaviour was the sweet and devoted Rottweiler.

It's difficult to pinpoint exactly when or why the breed was saddled with such a bad reputation. Perhaps some found their size intimidating? Fully grown males can tip the scales at 60 kilograms, with females only a little slighter at 48 kilograms, so they admittedly do have plenty of heft.

Perhaps their natural protective instincts, developed over millennia, made people wary. In Roman times, Rottweilers were used as herding and driving dogs, marching over the Alps with Roman legions, protecting both humans and livestock as they went. The modern-day Rottie was developed in the early twentieth century, and they were used widely in the both world wars as messenger, ambulance and guard dogs.

Unsurprisingly, with a drive to protect written in their DNA, Rottweilers have long been commonly used as guard dogs, not just for sheep and cattle, but property as well. The image of a snarling, salivating Rottie in a chain-link collar no doubt helped to perpetuate the idea of the breed being ill-tempered 'junkyard dogs'.

Growing up with Rottweilers on the rural outskirts of Canberra in the eighties, Jarrad Houghton was spared the myths and hysteria around the breed – he has only ever known them to be loving and loyal.

Jarrad and his two younger sisters grew up on a property at Hall, right on the New South Wales–ACT border, which his parents operated as an equestrian centre. As well as training dressage horses, they agisted other people's horses at the facility's twenty-plus stables.

Though he was surrounded by horses from birth, it was dogs that captured Jarrad's heart – not least because they're a lot less work. 'I'm the eldest, and there's an eight-year and eleven-year age gap to each of my sisters, so when I was younger I was responsible for a lot of the chores to do with the horses,' he says. 'I learned to ride, and I enjoy riding, but horses aren't really my thing. Being a young fella, I just enjoyed running around with the dogs. I was a long-distance athlete for many years, always running up and down the country roads, and the dogs would come with me.'

And there were a *lot* of dogs. They always had Rottweilers, but Jarrad also remembers his family as being the go-to adopters for canines at the local vet hospital that were looking for new homes.

'We took in a lot of animals, mostly smaller ones like fox terriers and things like that. We bought Rottweilers as our "dog of choice", but we usually had as many as four or more different dogs,' he recalls.

For Jarrad, the family Rotties were the consummate playmates: always up for a run, a game or a wrestle, and never nasty, no matter how boisterous the play.

'Even being young and roughhousing with them, they were quite gentle with me. They're very playful,' he says. 'I was blissfully unaware of their reputation as scary dogs. We didn't really watch TV on the farm, and when certain horror movies featuring the breed came out, I was too young to watch them anyway. I didn't become aware that they were viewed as anything other than a playful type of dog until much later in life.'

Ignorance may have been bliss for the young Jarrad, but plenty of other people had absorbed the message that Rottweilers were to be feared, including some visitors to the equestrian centre.

He remembers thinking it was 'a bit strange' when a new visitor would drive onto the property and act fearfully. 'They wouldn't get out of the car because of the dogs. But regulars who knew the dogs would often embrace them.'

On one occasion, a man who *did* get out of his vehicle was rewarded with a crash course in just how seriously Rottweilers take their role as guardians of their turf.

'We used to get our horse feed delivered. One day the delivery guy came out and we weren't home. He took a bale of hay into the feed shed, turned around and saw that the two Rotties had bailed him up.'

The dogs didn't lay a paw on the man, but they were adamant he would not be departing until a member of the family arrived to vouch for him.

'They just wouldn't let him leave. They didn't attack him or do anything outrageous, but if he tried to get out, they wouldn't let him. The poor guy was stuck in the feed shed for a couple of hours.'

It was a formative lesson for Jarrad in just how devoted Rotties are to their humans – even when their humans aren't there. Later, he would learn to apply that devotion to building an even stronger bond with his dogs.

'If you throw a ball for a Staffy, they'll run and get it, and they'll do that all day long. Rottweilers are a bit different. I noticed from a young age that if I ran towards one of the Rotties they would run away, but if I turned around and ran in the other direction they'd chase me,' he explains. 'I realised that, to build a good relationship with a Rottweiler, I couldn't play fetch in the traditional way. They want to have contact with their handler, so a game of tag or tug-of-war with a rope is better, because they feel more connected with you. That's true for many breeds.'

When he grew up and left home, Jarrad spent about five years without a dog – though visits back to the family property were always available when he felt the need to scratch that canine companion itch. Then, in the early 2000s, he met the woman who would later become his wife, and he became a doting 'stepdad' to her rescued bull terrier, Timmy.

'Timid Timmy', as he was known, was scared of most things. He was believed to have been subjected to some abuse in his younger years. He was extremely wary of men, so Jarrad knew that winning him over wouldn't be easy.

'It was suspected that he'd been abused by a man, and when I first met him, he would not come anywhere near me. He'd had a hard life, and he had quite a few scars on his face,' he says. But Jarrad worked hard to earn Timmy's trust. 'Within a few months we were the best of mates.'

Timmy reminded Jarrad of the joys of dog ownership, and when the old dog passed away it hit Jarrad hard. His grief was compounded by the end of his marriage. As he embarked on his newly single life, Jarrad knew he needed a four-legged friend of his own.

And, of course, he knew immediately that his new best friend had to be a Rottweiler.

Jarrad did his due diligence, searching high and low for a reputable breeder that either had puppies ready to go to their forever families or was planning a litter in the near future. In 2010, he eventually put his name on a waiting list with a breeder in Cooma, in New South Wales, 110 kilometres south of Canberra.

He was expecting a long wait; the breeder's current litter hadn't even arrived yet but all the puppies were already spoken for. But then came a stroke of luck: a buyer pulled out, leaving one female pup without a home to go to.

'She was the only puppy that didn't get sold and I was on the waiting list, so it was meant to be,' says Jarrad. He brought her home and called her Pepper. From the very start, he says, she was a typical female Rottweiler: protective, nurturing, instinctive and highly intelligent.

'She had quite a maternal instinct, so she was quite protective of me and my boys,' says Jarrad, who shares three sons with his former wife. 'I've noticed that difference between my male and female Rottweilers. Males will tend to approach someone whether they know them or not, but the females in some cases will refuse to meet. Pepper would sort of stand back and observe people. There were one or two people she met that she wasn't quite sure about, so she would just stay by my side.'

On one particular occasion, Pepper's instincts proved to be spot on. Jarrad fed her a raw diet comprising 80 per cent lean meat mixed with fruit and vegetables, plus 10 per cent offal and 10 per cent bone. The food was delivered to his home by the same man each time. Looking back, he remembers getting 'a bad vibe' from the guy, but he ignored it since their interactions were so brief.

Pepper, on the other hand, was not so quick to dismiss *her* gut instinct.

'One day he brought some new treats he was selling, this dried whitebait. He wanted to come into the house and meet Pepper, to try these new treats out on her.'

But Pepper wouldn't have a bar of the visitor. She flat out refused to approach the front door where the man stood.

Later, the man missed several scheduled deliveries. When Jarrad made enquiries, he learned he had been jailed for a violent assault. Pepper had clearly been all too aware that the delivery man was a bad egg.

But not long after Pepper joined the family, Jarrad really started to notice the prejudice against Rottweilers.

'Now that I'm older, I've seen some of the ways they're portrayed in movies – they're the bad guy, the junkyard dog.'

Pepper was a mother hen and an excellent judge of character, but not everyone was a fan. It frustrated him that the breed still hadn't managed to shake off the misconceptions that plagued it – many people were outright scared of Rotties, because they had never got to know one.

'One of my neighbours was an elderly lady and she would cross the road when she saw me walking with Pepper. I'd cross the road to meet her and introduce her to Pepper, and she would cross back to the other side. She used to call Pepper "Satan's dog".'

Some dog owners would be discouraged or disheartened by such a reaction, but not Jarrad. Instead, he doubled down and started searching for a second Rottie.

As luck would have it, the dog he chose proved exactly how gentle and protective Rottweilers are.

Many people like to celebrate their milestone birthdays by doing something big. They might jet off on the holiday of a lifetime, buy that dream car or designer handbag, or get the tattoo they've always wanted.

In March 2017, Jarrad marked his fortieth birthday with the arrival of a Rottweiler puppy.

He didn't actually plan for the pooch to be his birthday gift to himself – it just worked out that way. He had spent two years looking for the right breeder. 'If I'd found the right one when I was thirty-eight it would have been a thirty-eighth birthday gift.'

But there was still something very special about bringing home a perfect, wriggling bundle of fluff just in time to celebrate the big four-oh.

'It took a while to find the right dog, not just for breeding but one that would fit in with children. A well-bred dog with manners,' he says.

He named his new little mate Basil, and in no time at all Basil showed he was not only naturally well mannered, but smart as a whip to boot. Capitalising on Basil's high food and play drives, Jarrad set about training the young Rottie in all the obedience fundamentals, using voice commands as well as hand signals.

'One finger up is a sit, an open hand is a stay, closed fist is a drop, and as long as I'm within sight he will do that from the length of a football field away,' he explains. 'Having watched Mum train dressage horses, I took away many lessons on how to train animals. I thought it would be beneficial to have silent commands in noisy areas. It's also just cool to have a dog that knows hand signals!'

For some extra input, he even sent Basil to a professional trainer of Rottweilers and German shepherds. That trainer operates a boarding kennel and training facility on his farm, which is home to a large array of resident animals, so Basil has been behaviour tested with introductions to everything from cats and reactive dogs to ducks and alpacas – and has passed each one with flying colours.

'It was just to back up my own training. I wanted Basil to be bomb-proof. I'm not a professional trainer, so I took him to one.'

The result of all this focused training and hard work was that, by the time he was just nine months old, Basil was a confident, calm and compliant dog. And that was never more evident than on the night of 16 February 2018.

It was a balmy late summer evening in Canberra and Jarrad was rounding off a busy week with dinner at The Dock, a popular dog-friendly pub at Kingston, on the shores of Canberra's Lake Burley Griffin. Basil, as usual, was right by his side.

'He was nearly full grown, but mentally he was still quite young. I'd been taking him to different areas to train him and expose him to new sights and sounds,' he says. 'I took him for a walk around Lake Burley Griffin, near all the federal government buildings. After we finished our walk we went to The Dock and enjoyed a pizza and a beer.'

Suitably refreshed, the pair got ready to head home. The Dock is one of a plethora of bars and eateries lining a wide promenade in the Kingston Foreshore precinct. From there, steps lead down to a narrower second terrace, below which is a near two-metre drop into the lake, which remains icy cold even in the warmer months.

Jarrad and Basil set out for home along the top terrace, which took them past the other bustling restaurants.

Suddenly, Basil made a beeline straight for the water.

'He almost pulled my arm out of its socket trying to get to the water's edge!' Jarrad recalls. 'I thought it was a little odd. He was usually so well behaved. I figured he was just being an excitable young dog, so rather than fight him I thought, *I'll investigate what's got under his skin and turn this into a training exercise.* Instead of saying, "No, we're going this way," I just stayed relaxed and thought, *Okay, I'll come with you, and we'll take ten minutes to train in a different area.*'

He followed Basil down the steps to the lower terrace, planning to stop the eager dog there and drill him on his obedience commands.

But Basil showed no sign of slowing down. After leaping from the bottom step, he continued to pull Jarrad towards the water with every ounce of his strength.

'He was about to pull me over the edge, so I looked over. As I did, I saw a little hand sticking up.'

Unable to process what he was seeing in the murky water 2 metres below, for a split second Jarrad thought a mannequin had been tossed into the lake.

Then he realised the hand was real. Somebody was in the water.

And, judging by the tiny fingers, that somebody was a child.

Instantly, Jarrad leapt into action. He dropped Basil's leash and lay down on the concrete. His muscles strained as he stretched his arm down towards the surface of the lake.

'Half hanging over the edge of the terrace, I had just enough reach to grab her hand and pull her out,' he says.

The tiny, soaked figure now stood before him, shivering on the terrace. The eight-year-old girl was in such a state of shock, Jarrad says she scarcely 'knew what to say or think or do'.

He understood exactly how she felt in that moment.

'She hadn't been screaming. She wasn't treading water. There are ladders, but one was fifty metres one way and the other was fifty metres the other way – and she wasn't thinking about ladders anyway, she was just sinking. It all just happened so quickly. I was a bit stunned myself. I was just having dinner and a beer, training my dog, and all of a sudden this happens. I couldn't really believe it. I was just grateful she was alive.'

And he was grateful – *so* very grateful – for his big, exuberant Rottweiler.

People involved in near-death situations often say that it takes some time to really grasp how close they or somebody else came to losing their life. Not Jarrad – he understood immediately that Basil had saved the little girl's life. His dog was a hero.

In the aftermath of the near drowning, Basil was strangely calm. He stood quietly by Jarrad's side, perhaps taking a moment to enjoy the satisfaction of a job very well done.

'The whole reason he was so determined to get down to the water was because he knew something was up.

With my mere human senses, I'd heard nothing, and in the dusk light I couldn't see very well. But Basil must have seen or heard something – perhaps he heard her splashing in the water, or calling out.'

But Basil didn't just hear a noise or catch a flash of movement from the corner of his eye, he somehow instantly knew that it wasn't a good situation. He knew that something was amiss and felt duty bound to investigate.

How did he know? It's a question Jarrad still asks himself often.

'I hate to even talk about it, but I would have given her another ten seconds and the story in the newspaper the next day would have been very different,' he says. 'Had I been by myself I never would have known. I would have just kept walking up by the restaurants. And if Basil had somehow got down to the water by himself, even if he'd jumped in, how would either of them have got out? I was in the right place at the right time, and I'm very glad I listened to Basil and decided to go with him rather than forcing my will on him.'

As the reality of the situation started to settle in, more questions arose. Who was this little girl? And where was her family?

She led Jarrad and Basil to one of the restaurants on the top terrace. It wasn't a dog-friendly establishment – ironically, Basil wasn't even allowed inside with the little girl whose life he'd saved.

'One of the staff came out and I told them that I wanted to make sure I handed the child over to the parents. I didn't want to just leave her in the restaurant by herself. Was that even the right restaurant? I wanted to make sure they were reunited.'

Eventually, the girl's parent emerged. If Jarrad had expected thanks, or perhaps a pat on the head for Basil, he was about to be disappointed.

'Her parent seemed taken aback. They said, "Who are you and why is my child wet?" They didn't really know what to make of the situation, even though I tried to explain it. After they were reunited, I went on my merry way.'

As the evening wore on, Jarrad pondered the strangeness of the situation. A father himself, he would not have felt comfortable letting his sons play so close to deep water without supervision, especially in an area emblazoned with signs urging parents to keep a close eye on their children. But he also knew from his own childhood how easy it is for kids to find themselves in trouble. 'Kids will be kids sometimes. With my farm upbringing, I can understand how they get themselves into dangerous situations.'

More than anything, however, he was immensely proud of young Basil. He couldn't help but think about the many times people had actively avoided crossing paths with both Basil and Pepper, when 60-kilogram Basil was capable of such a selfless and caring act.

He wished more people were able to see how gentle and protective Rottweilers were. So he jumped on social media and said so.

'Later that night, I put a post on a Facebook group for Canberra residents saying, "Hey, next time you see me walking with my two Rottweilers, come and say hi, because tonight Basil saved someone."'

His intention had been simply to show his fellow Canberrans that Rotties are wonderful dogs, but the post quickly attracted a *lot* of attention. 'I was just trying to reassure people that we're approachable. That just because people see two big dogs, they don't need to cross the road. Maybe I was naive, but it went quite viral.'

He was dismayed to see that many of the responses to his post were critical of the little girl's parents, berating them for what they saw as inadequate supervision. Jarrad felt compelled to defend them, since they couldn't defend themselves. 'I did stick up for them, saying, "This is not what this post is about. Let's lay off – we want a good news story, not a public flogging." I just tried to make it all about Basil.'

Basil's heroic act soon came to the attention of the *Canberra Times* newspaper, which published a front-page article about the vigilant pooch the next day. Over the coming weeks Basil made headlines worldwide. Jarrad now has that first story framed, as a lasting memento.

The little girl's family were also tracked down and asked to participate in photoshoots and television interviews with Jarrad and Basil, but they declined. Jarrad was a little disappointed – he would have liked to have the opportunity to do some more Rottweiler myth-busting with a larger audience – but he understood their decision.

'It would have been nice to be able to promote Rottweilers on that kind of platform, to say, "All dogs are okay – it's the people that own and train them that can sometimes be the problem." But the main thing was that the girl was alive.'

All thanks to Basil. While the brave dog may not have had the chance to reconnect with the child whose life he saved, Jarrad made sure he knew he was appreciated.

'I made a bit of a fuss of him and took him out for a steak. He was blissfully unaware. He was just happy to keep going out for steaks!'

The 'coolest thing', says Jarrad, was that Basil was also honoured with a special award from the Rottweiler Club of NSW, which recognised that his actions and the subsequent coverage had done wonders to highlight the breed's many wonderful qualities. It was the first time in Australia that a Rottie had received such an award.

And there was no doubt that Basil's heroism changed a lot of minds about Rottweilers – at least in Jarrad's neighbourhood.

'He became the talk of the town for a little while. Everywhere we went, he would get recognised. It was a stark contrast, because before this happened I'd take Basil and Pepper walking and eighty per cent of people would not come near us,' he says. 'After the rescue, ninety-five per cent of people recognised him and wanted to hug him and shake his paw and give him pats.'

Always on the lookout for training opportunities, Jarrad was sure to take advantage of these interactions. 'I make sure that in my handler's bag I carry a lot of cheese with me. It was a good opportunity to give people a cube of cheese and say, "Here you go, tell him to sit, or use a hand signal."'

Jarrad and Basil were also inundated with free products like kennels and coats, as well as offers of various grooming services from local businesses and even a $300 pet photography session. The generosity was entirely unexpected, and Jarrad not only didn't need many of the items flooding in, he also didn't feel quite right about accepting them while so many other deserving dogs went without.

'I was grateful that there were people out there who were so generous, but I felt a bit embarrassed about it,' he confesses.

He had long been thinking about setting up a group on Facebook that would allow dog owning Canberrans to meet up with people from their area and exercise their canine companions.

'I approached all these businesses that had reached out to me and asked if they would be open to me paying these items forward. I wanted to run a competition each month to give away the things they'd wanted to give me, as a means of bringing people together.'

All the business owners agreed, and Canberra Pack Walks was born. More than thirty people and their dogs attended the first prize giveaway night, at the dog-friendly pub Capital Brewing Co.

'It was important to me to promote local businesses that had recognised Basil's good deed and wanted to support him,' says Jarrad.

Sadly, 2018 wasn't all full of good news for Jarrad and Basil. In September, beautiful Pepper – the sweet, motherly dog that had reignited Jarrad's love of Rottweilers – passed away with bone cancer at the age of eight. Her loss devastated Jarrad, and Basil, too, was completely heartbroken without his mate.

'Basil was still quite young, not even a year old, and he and Pepper had grown so close. He howled at the moon for several weeks after she passed. He would just stand on the back deck and howl at the sky,' he says. 'It was pretty hard. I ended up taking a few weeks off work and prioritised hanging out with him.'

Fortunately, another friend was waiting in the wings to help Basil process his grief: a ten-year-old border collie, Jess.

'When they were first introduced, Jess was quite dog reactive. We very slowly went walking together, but apart – we would have a football field between us and Jess would bark at Basil from the other side.'

It wasn't too long before playful, charming Basil convinced Jess to give him a chance.

'Slowly but surely Jess came around, and now they're almost inseparable. They follow each other around and play together. They eat together, sleep together, and generally run amok together.'

And it seems Jess is the boss in the relationship, despite being considerably smaller.

'It's funny watching them together, because Basil weighs close to sixty kilograms and Jess is only twenty-five kilograms, but he is quite submissive with her. He'll roll over and she'll stand over him and mouth at his face and his feet,' he says. 'I could watch them for hours. They just adore each other.'

It's not hard to see why Jess adores Basil. It's not hard to see why *anyone* adores Basil. He's a faithful companion with a huge heart and an indomitable spirit. He's a wonderful ambassador for his breed, and he's a bona fide lifesaver. And that makes him pretty amazing.

Lexi

The ute-driving dog

Before we dive in, let's just clear something up. Lexi the Jack Russell terrier can drive a car, but she cannot actually *drive a car*.

You might see Lexi behind the wheel of a vehicle, but fear not: you won't see her roaring down the freeway at 110 kilometres per hour. She's not going to be doing doughnuts in the paddock and she will never dent your bumper in a supermarket car park.

Lexi's 'driving' career has always been about making people smile, not getting from point A to point B. Nobody is advocating for dogs to become licensed drivers, and the everyday pet owner should categorically *not* try this at home. Just in case anybody has their pen poised to write a stern letter to the publisher of this book.

With that out of the way: meet Cameron Zschech. The 21-year-old from Hamilton in south-west Victoria is the wearer of many hats: sheep farmer's son, forestry worker, talented amateur photographer, creator of funny videos, dog lover. Cam is also a bit of a larrikin.

A larrikin, for those that are not familiar with Australian slang, is somebody who doesn't take life too seriously. While never disrespectful, a larrikin is irreverent, a bit cheeky, and always looking for the next opportunity to have a laugh.

That's Cam to a tee – and it's also a handy descriptor for his sassy canine sidekick, Lexi.

Though Cam's been surrounded by dogs all his life, Lexi is the first bona fide pet pooch he's ever owned.

'Growing up on a sheep farm, I've always had sheep-dogs. We've always had at least one kelpie at home. But I've always wanted a little dog as a pet rather than a working dog,' Cam says. 'A sheepdog is still a pet in a sense, but it's different. The kelpies never bring toys back to you. Well, mine don't!'

The incumbent farm dog, a kelpie named Pippa, was well past retirement age for a working dog. She still enjoyed pitching in occasionally, but she was becoming less playful than she'd ever been, which wasn't a whole lot to begin with.

'She's probably around fifteen years old now, so she doesn't do much. She's got a few spots in the yard where she likes to just sit and sleep, so most of the time she does that,' he says. 'She's not high energy anymore. She likes to chase the sheep and then go and relax.'

Cam spent years lobbying his dad, Ian, to let him have a pet dog, to no avail. But when he met his partner, Chloe, in 2020, he suddenly had double the pester power.

'Chloe helped me convince Dad, and finally he agreed to let us get a little Jack Russell terrier,' he says. Not that he was necessarily looking for a JRT specifically – Cam's only real requirement was that his new canine companion be smaller than a kelpie.

He and Chloe got in touch with a handful of breeders of different dog breeds and were shocked to discover that pedigree JRT puppies cost upwards of $2000. It was out of reach for Cam, who at that time was working weekdays in forestry in Portland, about an hour away from Hamilton, and then working for his dad on the farm on weekends.

For a while it looked like Cam's long-held dream might have to wait a little longer. Then, in January 2021, he spied a classified advertisement in the local newspaper. 'This fella's Jack Russell had had puppies and he was selling them for eight-hundred dollars each. We went to this little farm about twenty minutes away, near Coleraine, to meet them. There were four or five of them there and he said, "Take your pick."'

Cam and Chloe spent time with each of the puppies and eventually chose a sweet little female that seemed slightly less frenetic than her littermates. 'We chose the quiet one in the corner because we wanted a quiet dog,' he says.

It took less than a week for them to realise the dog, who they had named Lexi, wasn't the shy and retiring type after all.

'She's not very quiet – she played a bit of a trick on us. She's never calm. She's got lots of energy and she's always running around, flat out,' says Cam with a laugh. 'Lexi just wants to play all the time. You could throw a milk carton and she'll bring it back to you.'

In fact, Lexi has been known to become quite irate when she can't find a willing playmate.

'She's got this one frisbee toy that she loves. We'll be sitting on the couch at night and she'll grab it and come and shake her head and try to hit us with the frisbee to make us throw it,' he says. 'She gets really annoyed if we won't throw stuff for her.'

The breed's playful nature is quite literally in their DNA. Originating from dogs bred and used by the Reverend John 'Jack' Russell in the early 1800s, JRTs were initially used in fox hunting – they're working dogs at heart. Their compact size, courage, tenacity and indefatigable energy meant they were perfect for squeezing into fox dens and making their quarry bolt out. Later, as the related fox terrier became more popular among fox hunters, the JRT was widely used in hunting other ground-dwelling animals, such as badgers, groundhogs and otters. They also became – and remain – a common sight on farms, where they can be relied upon to chase away rats and other small vermin.

Over time, JRTs also became sought-after as pets – in 2021, they were Australia's ninth most-popular dog breed, with 579 registered litters bred nationally. With their exuberance and high drive, they are much-loved by active owners, though they can become destructive if not properly stimulated. Let's just say that, if left to entertain themselves, they'll create their own fun.

In a nutshell, whether working, playing, or just generally creating chaos, JRTs are dogs that always want to be *doing*. Occasionally that go-getting spirit leads them into trouble, as Lexi discovered after relocating to Tasmania with Cam and Chloe.

The couple upped sticks in June 2022 after Cam secured a job transfer to Burnie, a port city on the north-west coast of Tasmania, where experienced forestry workers are in high demand and short supply. One-year-old Lexi also made the move, of course, as did Chloe's JRT, Pippa (not to be confused with the Zschech family's kelpie of the same name).

In Hamilton, Lexi had become familiar with night-time visits to the farm from curious wildlife, including kanagroos and possums. But Tasmania's nocturnal animals are a different breed entirely.

'The first week we moved down to Tassie, it was about six-thirty at night and we were walking from the car to the house when Lexi suddenly disappeared. We were calling and calling her, but she wouldn't come back,' Cam says.

The area behind his and Chloe's house is farmland, meaning there was a very large – and very dark – area in which Lexi could have become lost.

They got straight back in the car and hit the road to search for her. 'She was out in someone's paddock. We'd hear her every now and then, but we had no clue where she was. We were driving around, calling her, but we just couldn't find her.'

After about 30 minutes that 'felt like forever', Cam and Chloe were forced to concede defeat. They knew they were unlikely to find Lexi in the pitch black of night. They would have to resume their search at first light, and hope their adventurous little dog was wily enough to avoid disaster until then.

Dejected, they returned home and parked the car once more. As they walked towards the house, however, a spine-chilling noise suddenly erupted from the darkness. It was a sound unlike any they had ever heard before – a menacing mix of a raspy scream and high-pitched howl – but they knew immediately what it was.

'Our neighbour had told us that Tasmanian devils lived around the property and would come out at night. This one was right near the house,' says Cam. 'We heard this awful screaming noise and both Chloe and I had the same thought: *I hope it hasn't attacked the dog.*'

Tasmanian devils are known to be solitary, territorial animals that aggressively guard their food. They make a variety of sounds, often when feeding at night, ranging from growls and grunts to the loud shrieks and screams Cam and Chloe heard.

After several tense minutes, during which Cam began to fear the worst, Lexi suddenly emerged from the gloom and strolled nonchalantly towards the house. He has no doubt she encountered a devil that night, but somehow, thankfully, she emerged unscathed.

'She sounds pretty smart, until you meet her,' he jokes.

It wasn't the first time Lexi had thrown caution to the wind in pursuit of adventure. Just a couple of months earlier, Lexi had decided to put the *joy* in 'joyride', bringing much-needed smiles to the faces of hundreds of thousands of people.

It is something of a crashing understatement to say the whole world has had a tough few years. The COVID-19 pandemic has claimed more than 6.5 million lives since the first cases were recorded in late 2019. At the time of writing, more than 550 million people have been diagnosed with the virus.

Lockdowns aimed at limiting transmission of coronavirus decimated the global economy, leading to widespread business closures, unemployment, panic buying and food shortages. Border closures meant many families were unable to see each other in-person for up to two years.

For a long time, it felt like the pandemic had brought out the very worst in humanity. There didn't seem to be much at all to smile about. But in the midst of all the doom and gloom there was, of course, still plenty of positive news. The Himalayas became visible from certain parts of India for the first time in decades thanks to the dramatic improvement in air quality. Australian researchers reported that early trials of a new vaccine for blood cancers had shown promising signs. Conservation scientists announced that, since 1993, forty-eight species of birds and mammals had been brought back from the edge of extinction. A dog named Drools found his forever home after spending 729 days in a shelter. The cast of *Friends* reunited for a one-off special.

As well as the headline-grabbing good news stories, heart-warming social media content played a big part in cheering people up. We were collectively looking for laughs, and we turned to the internet to find them – Cam included. But he wasn't just consuming content, he was creating it.

A keen photographer, while still living in Victoria Cam taught himself to take spectacular photos of the night sky. He sometimes sent his shots to the ABC South West Vic Facebook page, where the national broadcaster posted local content for people in the region to enjoy. And, like most doting dog owners, he took videos of his canine companion almost every day. One day, in May 2022, Cam's creative spirit and the reach of social media came together in the most uplifting way.

Cam had been diagnosed with COVID-19 and couldn't go to work in Portland, despite feeling reasonably well.

So he decided to get a jump on some of the farm chores he would usually tackle at the weekend.

He loaded Lexi into the passenger seat of his ute and the pair set out to shift a mob of sheep from one paddock to another. But Lexi wasn't content to remain a passenger for long.

'She normally just sits on the passenger seat. She'll put her paws up on the window or the dash and see what's going on,' Cam says. 'On this day there were some sheep on the driver's side, so she jumped into my lap and put her paws up on the steering wheel. I thought, *That looks pretty funny.*'

The next day they headed out together again and Lexi repeated her new trick. Thinking on his feet, Cam grabbed his mobile phone and shot a quick video that made it look like Lexi was driving.

'Then I thought, *I reckon I can make this even better.*'

When working by himself in a flat paddock, Cam will sometimes put the ute into first gear and let it crawl along at low speed while he walks beside the vehicle, distributing hay for the sheep from the tray. This time, he decided to try it while sitting in the passenger seat with Lexi at the wheel.

'I put the ute in first gear so it would just idle along, then moved Lexi into the driver's seat. Straight away she jumped up and put her paws on the steering wheel again.'

That was a cute video in itself, but the scope of Cam's cinematic vision was about to get even better.

The sheep that were in front of the vehicle suddenly moved en masse. Ever the vigilant hunting dog, Lexi didn't take her eyes off them. She turned her head and leaned in the direction they were heading, which made it appear as though she was trying to turn the steering wheel.

Cam captured it all on his phone and enjoyed a good chuckle. Later that day he showed the video to Chloe and Ian, thinking they might get a kick out of 'Lexi the driving dog'.

'I thought it was pretty funny, but I think every little video that I make is pretty interesting. Then I'll show my girlfriend and my dad and they'll just think it's silly,' he says.

To his surprise, his hard-to-please critics thought this video was worthy of being seen by a wider audience. 'I showed it to them and they both said, "Send this to the ABC South West Vic Facebook page."'

He did just that, figuring the sweet video might be seen by a few hundred locals, the way his night-sky photography was.

Cam was entirely unprepared, then, for what actually happened next.

'They rang me up and said they wanted to do an interview with me for the radio,' he says, a note of disbelief in his voice. 'I said, "Are you joking?"'

They were not joking. The ABC was in fact very serious about developing a story they recognised as a much-needed moment of levity in what had become an almost invariably negative news cycle.

It sounded like a laugh, so Cam agreed to the interview. Then he did another. And another.

'The ABC gave me a list of videos that they wanted me to make, showing Lexi in different situations, so they could put it all together. A week or two later they put it on TV,' says Cam. 'Everyone at work thought it was pretty funny. She's definitely had a bit of publicity – she's still only a year old, so she's done pretty well in her life.'

Soon, Lexi was even charming people on the other side of the planet – and Cam was having plenty of cheeky fun with his dog's newfound international stardom.

'I got an email from a news company in Finland. They were asking me things like, "It's been a couple of weeks since Lexi started driving – how has she improved? What kinds of jobs have you got her doing?"' he explains. 'I wrote back, "We have enrolled Lexi in a vigorous seven-day driving course and she's doing really good. We're hoping to get her to the stage where she can drive into town and get the milk and bread. We're just waiting on council permits."'

Every time he agreed to talk to another media outlet about Lexi's skills behind the wheel, he assumed that would be the end of it. Instead, each media appearance seem to make more and more people happy.

He next received a call from a journalist from Nine Network's nightly magazine show *A Current Affair*. They wanted to cover Lexi's antics and were proposing they'd come up from Melbourne to see her in action.

'That's a four-hour drive. I thought, *I hope they're not expecting too much*. I said, "You do realise she can't actually drive? She's a dog, you understand?"' says Cam.

They confirmed that they understood that Lexi wasn't putting the pedal to the metal on the open road, but they wanted to meet her anyway.

Lexi eventually also made online and broadcast news headlines in the United Kingdom, Canada and the United States. Delighted as he was that people all over the world shared his opinion that his dog was pretty special, Cam admits he found Lexi's sudden fame a little overwhelming.

'At the time there were so many people calling and messaging me that I probably didn't reply to three-quarters of them. With the forestry work that I do, I'm working twelve-hour days, five days a week. When I get home I don't feel like ringing people – I just want to sleep,' he says. 'These journalists all had my phone number and they'd be calling me throughout the day. They'd all want to talk to me for half an hour, and I just haven't got that time to talk to them. I ended up just not answering my phone during the day.'

But the Lexi frenzy eventually eased off, and by then Cam had other things to think about – namely his and Chloe's big move to Tasmania. The pair share a long-held desire to see as much of the world as possible, and they were thrilled to land an opportunity to kick off their travels with an extended stay on the Apple Isle.

There was never any question that both Pippa and Lexi would be moving with them. They will also come along for the ride when Cam and Chloe embark on the next leg of their adventure: a trip around Australia. Lexi, however, will be firmly in the passenger seat rather than behind the wheel when they eventually hit the road.

Pippa may be hoping that Lexi's relentless puppy energy may have calmed down a bit by then. 'She's a couple of years old and Lexi is still a puppy, so she's still really energetic,' says Cam. 'She's always trying to play with Pippa, and poor Pippa just wants to lie there, sleeping! But having them both means they can keep each other company when we do go around Australia.'

And while Cam hopes to capture many more videos of his beloved canine companion being adorable and hilarious in the years to come, he's realistic about Lexi's chances of going viral a second time (and would be more than happy if she doesn't).

'The thing is, I don't have that many good ideas of things to get her to do! The driving idea just happened. I didn't think of it, Lexi just jumped up there and did it. It was one of those random things,' he says. 'If I tried to think of something for her to do, it wouldn't end up being that funny – but if I just take a video of her doing something, that's when the magic happens. You've just got to let it happen.'

That's exactly what makes Lexi an amazing Aussie dog. In fact, it's what makes *all* dogs amazing. She didn't *plan* to make thousands of people love her. It wasn't her intention to make us all smile at a time when we really, really needed it. She couldn't possibly have known the entire world was feeling down in the dumps. As far as Lexi was concerned, that day was perfection: the sun was shining, her owner was unexpectedly at home with her, and they were out in the fresh air, spending time together.

Lexi just wanted a closer look at the sheep in the paddock, and the easiest way to make that happen was to jump into the driver's seat of the ute, so that's what she did.

A dog couldn't contrive to win somebody over if they tried. Dogs simply exist, and we adore them for it.

Bruno

The accidental explorer

Author's note

A *funny thing happened when I sat down to write about Emma Broe and her psychiatric support dog, Bruno. I found I couldn't do it.*

No *matter how hard I tried (and how many discarded drafts I tossed viciously into the bin), I just could not properly encapsulate exactly what Bruno means to Emma, and vice versa. It was beyond me to describe the gut-wrenching agony she felt when he went missing. I couldn't explain the love and support of the Whiskey's Wish community that cocooned Emma as she searched for him. And I had no chance of finding words to match the real-life drama of Emma's literally death-defying efforts to find her beloved boy.*

I *simply cannot tell the astonishing story of this remarkable woman and her amazing dog any better than*

Emma tells it herself. So I'm leaving it to Emma – with added insight into the rescue efforts from Whiskey's Wish trainer Linda Mair – to do just that.

Here, in Emma's own words, is the tale of her and Bruno.

Please note that this story contains descriptions of suicidal ideation and the symptoms of PTSD. If you or a loved one need support, you can call Lifeline on 13 11 14 or chat online at lifeline.org.au.

Emma Broe

I live in Far North Queensland, on an 8-acre property near Cairns. In 2012 I joined the State Emergency Service (SES) in Cairns and worked extensively for them as a volunteer in a whole range of roles.

It wasn't until 2017 that Chronic Post Traumatic Stress Disorder began to affect me. I'd been deployed south at the tail end of Cyclone Debbie, which devastated the area. I was sent down to set up and man a police road-block. It was so windy, I was having to put sandbags on my feet to hold myself down.

I was diagnosed with post-traumatic stress disorder (PTSD). People don't understand what PTSD is and how much it takes away from your life. It has become a buzz-word recently. I even had a colleague of mine say, 'I've got PTSD, too' and when I said, 'I'm terribly sorry, I hope you're coping,' he replied, 'Yes, my accounts were late.'

When I was diagnosed, I had a German shepherd called Oberon. I've always had German shepherds – my gran had them when I was growing up, and I've always loved them.

My dogs have always had names that have included the word 'bear' in different languages. I had a beautiful long-coat German shepherd called Bijan (Bear for short) which is Persian for hero. Oberon comes from the Germanic and means royal bear.

Oberon was my life. He helped me through so much. He instinctively knew when I was happy and when I was sad or having a panic attack. He was very intuitive. I don't think I would be here without him.

I could never find another German shepherd to be a companion for him. Oberon never used to bark, but one day in early 2017 he started barking really loudly and really excitedly at a German shepherd walking past my property. I thought, *That's weird*. Every morning for a month he would bark his head off at this dog. The other dog would bark back a couple of times and then carry on with her walk.

On the morning of 27 May, around 6 a.m., I was sitting on the verandah and Oberon came over and started nudging me. He was only eight or nine years old, but I could tell he wasn't well. I started panicking and said, 'No, you can't go, you just can't.'

He weighed 48 kilograms – heavier than me; I'm only 163 centimetres tall – but I picked him up, put him in my ute and went to the vet. I lay down with him on the table and he was licking my hand as if to give me permission to go forward. I sang 'Hush Little Baby'. He listened until the very last word and then he gave me a big kiss and died. There was no reason for it.

I came home and didn't know what the hell to do. I felt that if I didn't have my boy, I didn't have anything. I was utterly distraught. I also had a terrier, Harvey, and he was desperately sad. I couldn't cope, and in my state of panic I thought, *I've got to find another German shepherd, now.*

I started looking up breeders, thinking there was never going to be anyone in Cairns, and suddenly there was. His advert stated that he'd just had a litter of four boys and four girls. Ideally I wanted a boy, but I really wasn't fussed. The pups had been born exactly ten days before Oberon died.

I rang the breeder and left a message saying, 'This is the situation – I've just lost my dog and I am absolutely anxious to have another.'

In the meantime I rang up Oberon's breeder, who lives way down south. She was going to have a litter in three months. To me that was way too far down the line.

Meanwhile, my mobile phone was ringing. It went to voicemail, then rang three more times. When I listened to the message it was the local breeder, Phil. He said, 'Yes, the pups haven't been allocated, give me a call back.'

It turned out we were neighbours: if you'd cut a tree down, I could have seen his back garden from my house. Phil's dog, Kenya, was the dog that Oberon had barked at every morning, and she was pregnant. Phil said, 'I wondered why that German shepherd was always barking.'

I went to Phil's house, literally just around the corner. He took me to see Kenya, but said, 'Don't go in.' New mothers can be very protective. A dog who's just had pups – they were only two weeks old – would usually never leave them to come to a human, but Kenya jumped out of her box and came straight to me, picking up her favourite crocodile toy on the way. She rolled onto her back and wanted her tummy scratched.

I started visiting the puppies once a week. On my fourth visit, they were up and running around, falling over on their stumpy legs. One little brown boy ran towards me and jumped into my lap. Mum would normally have come and retrieved him, but instead she came and jumped in too. He was only four weeks old and already jumping all over me. I knew he was the dog for me. I decided to call him Piccolo Orsetto Bruno, which means little brown bear cub in Italian.

The next time I visited, there were some other people there looking at the puppies. They were quite snooty and nasty. As I watched Bruno charge off to the bottom of the garden, this woman said, 'Which puppy are you having?'

I pointed him out and said, 'That one.'

She said, 'Oh, *brown boy*,' really disdainfully.

And who was the one playing the idiot ham at that moment? Bruno. He was trying to bite a root. Another puppy came along and threw soil at him and he just stood there, blinking.

He's my tenth German shepherd. Every one has been beautiful; I don't compare one with the others. Oberon was one of a kind, but with Bruno the mould broke. Oberon was my heart, but there was something completely and utterly different about Bruno from the moment I met him. That dog knows me better than I know myself.

Bruno has enabled me to go out and about. He's my right-hand man; we go everywhere together. I hadn't been to a restaurant in five years when I first got him. I couldn't go into a shopping centre at all. I would just panic and come out. He has opened up the world for me. He is my lifeline. He's the reason I'm here and the reason why I stay. Many times I was going to give up, but I stay for him.

Bruno has picked up all Oberon's traits, beyond reason. His eyes are identical to Oberon's. They're really, really big and brown. I would stare into Oberon's eyes all the time. Bruno has more insight than Oberon, but maybe I've got more insight into my own behaviour as well.

Bruno is a buffoon. He bounces on the spot and barks in this really high, shrill voice. He'll come to me at five minutes to six o'clock and say, *It actually is dinner time, you know.*

As he was growing up, I was trying to train him and not getting anywhere. He was doing all these naughty things and I was laughing. I hired a professional trainer and she said, 'He's intelligent but he won't respond to training.'

I was very lucky to work with a colleague whose husband was part of Whiskey's Wish, a Brisbane-based charity that provides service dog training and assistance to veterans, first responders and correctional officers suffering from PTSD and service-related injuries. It was started by Scott Jackman, an army veteran, and his wife, Liz, in memory of Scott's service dog Whiskey. My colleague said, 'You're a first responder with the SES, so you'd be eligible to join Whiskey's Wish and train Bruno as a service dog.'

I applied when Bruno was about eighteen months old, but I remember thinking there was absolutely no way I was going to be accepted. I'm not like soldiers who come home from war and have this enormous trauma. But I was accepted and told that as long as I had a psychologist to back me up, and as long as Bruno passed a temperament and behaviour test, we could start training.

Because they weren't quite ready for us to start, and I needed to get my evidence together, I started training privately with Linda Mair from Canine Training School. She is the trainer for Whiskey's Wish in Cairns.

I said to Linda, 'I am really trying to do this basic training with him, but all he's doing is jumping up and down like a carousel pony and walking backwards.' I stupidly taught him to walk backwards when he was a puppy.

She said, 'Have you ever stopped to think that maybe he's doing it to make you laugh because that's what he wants you to do?'

On the day of his behavioural assessment with Linda, I said, 'Please don't let me down, mate. You've really got to get it together and be sensible just for half an hour.' I'd never met Linda before and I was a bit anxious. We were walking over to her and I was saying to him, 'Slowly,' and he actually held back. I said, 'Sit,' and he sat down. I said, 'Bruno, down,' and he just lay down. I thought, *You little so-and-so, you've never done this in your life, even when I've pleaded with you to do it!*

Linda said, 'You've passed, you work really well together.'

We officially became a Whiskey's Wish team in 2019. That's when the mayhem started!

One of the things Bruno is trained to do for me is act as a buffer between me and other people. I don't like people encroaching upon my space because I feel hemmed in and start to panic. He doesn't become aggressive when people get too close, but he'll stand right by my side, looking at me and looking at the person, as if to say, *Are you okay, Mum?* If I say no, he steers me away. He actually started doing it without training, but I like to pretend I trained him to do it.

When my PTSD causes me to disassociate, which is very often, Bruno becomes very tactile. He will nudge me and if I don't respond he'll put a paw on my leg. If I don't respond to that, he'll use both paws, and if I still don't respond he'll lean in very close, put his head on mine and breathe very heavily.

It happened once when I was cleaning the bath – I crashed down and gave myself a concussion. When I came to, it had been a while, because it was dark. Bruno was standing with two feet on me in the bath, looking at me.

As well as PTSD, I have a condition called functional neurological disorder, which is like a loose feeling in my left-hand side. I fall over a lot, and Bruno is trained to act as my brace. He can sense when I'm about to fall and will brace himself against me. He'll lead me over to a chair so I can sit down.

He knows he's special to me. He's my heart dog, end of story. He always lies about a metre away from me, but his body is always facing me so that even if he's asleep he's 'looking' at me.

We live on a highway, but my property is tucked away. I also have two beautiful female Malinois, Arya and Mooch. Every morning we leave the girls at home, and I take my cup of coffee and walk one of the paddocks with Bruno. He'll be off-lead because he just trots along beside me. We look at plants and just chew that fat.

There is a quarry near me and trucks are always going up and down the highway. On Australia Day in 2022, Bruno and I were enjoying our morning walk when this truck came thundering down. I was aware of it because it was going so fast. There's a dip in the road and if trucks come down too fast – sometimes even cars – they will hit the road. The air brakes were going, and I started freaking out. Bruno was picking up on that. Then the truck blew a tyre and I lost it. I hit the ground.

Bruno is the most stoic dog anyone could meet. He once had an injury where the vets had to staple his head together, and he just sat there with no pain relief. But from my position on the ground, all I could see was Bruno's backside, bolting away in absolute terror. He was just going so fast.

I pulled myself sort of together and charged off towards the last place I'd seen him going, which was towards the creek behind my house. I carried on along the creek, but there was no sign of him anywhere. The creek runs parallel to the highway and then goes under the road. It's a perpetual creek, so it's always flowing, and it's usually about ankle deep. It's the most amazing sound from the house.

Bruno adores water. If he gets bored or knows that I've been sidetracked, he'll go off for a swim in the creek. I kept walking along the creek, calling for him, but figured he'd gone to have a play and would come home when he was good and ready.

Then the weather started changing. By the afternoon, the creek was getting deeper because of rain further north. Then the rain hit my place and got worse and worse and worse until the creek was a raging torrent. By the next day I was wading through chest-deep water on my search. I started to think it was going to be a case of finding Bruno, but not alive.

Linda Mair

As the trainer for Whiskey's Wish here in Cairns, I've known Bruno and Emma right from the start of their journey.

I didn't become aware of Bruno being missing right away. One of the other girls in our Whiskey's Wish team, Sarah, lives nearby, and Emma called her first when Bruno didn't come home. Sarah contacted me towards the end of the second day.

This dog is smart. We all knew that. He's used to being in the bush because Emma has always lived in remote areas. Initially we thought, *He'll come back*. We suspected Bruno had probably crossed the creek, because he's known to like having a swim. But the rain got us worried. There was also concern about how far he'd travelled. When they get a severe fright like Bruno had, dogs can just run and run and run.

We had a massive amount of rain on the third night. There was serious concern that he wouldn't be able to get back across the creek – and that if he tried, he wouldn't make it. Getting across the creek to try to find him, which Emma and Sarah had been doing, became impossible. Was he sitting somewhere out there in the torrential rain? Had he tried to cross the creek and drowned?

Sarah, Liz Jackman and I were posting all over social media, appealing for anyone who might have seen Bruno to get in touch. A lady who had been a client of mine contacted me and said she'd been up near the Davies Creek Mountain Bike Park on Australia Day afternoon and had seen a dog that looked like Bruno in the company of another dog.

It was a long way from where Emma lost him – it seemed like an impossible distance for Bruno to have travelled. He would have had to go through miles of bush. But we were grasping at straws, because how often does someone see a German shepherd running around in the bush? The fact that this dog was apparently with another dog threw us, too. We thought, *Has he picked up a farm dog on the way?* There's also a lot of dingos up there.

Together with my daughter, I went up to see Emma, because I needed to give her a hug. By this point I was frightened and heartbroken. I was thinking, *If we can't find this dog, what's going to happen to my darling Emma?*

The next day, myself and my friend Jess, who runs North Queensland Animal Rescue, went up at seven o'clock in the morning. Emma wanted to go to where this German shepherd had been sighted and then backtrack through the bush into the back of her property. Emma is a highly decorated SES volunteer – if you're going to get lost in the bush, Emma is the person you want walking beside you – but we didn't want her to go out there on her own.

There had been no confirmed sightings of Bruno since he had disappeared. We'd left signs up all around the creek, and at all the service stations, but we wanted to go up there for peace of mind. We went up there for half a day and covered all the ground we could in cars. There were places Emma wanted to go into and we had to say, 'We can't physically drive you into there.'

There were also friends of Sarah's who were mountain bike people, and there were people up there using drones. We had the word out through every ounce of social media that could be relevant for that area. One of the Whiskey's Wish girls got on to Triple M and it went out on the radio. I'd even spoken to the blokes at the quarry and they assured me that Bruno could not have got in there unless he'd walked in the front gate past their office.

Sometime around the 31st, so four days into the search, there was another contact. A lady messaged to say that her son was driving back from Mareeba late at night in the heavy rain and saw two German shepherds standing at the top of a driveway, not that far from where Emma lives. It turned out to be Tichum Creek Coffee Farm and the lady who owns it does have two German shepherds, so that was a dead end.

On 2 February, the same lady rang Sarah and said that the old German shepherd that had been spotted on Australia Day had turned up at her property and she had caught it. I got a text message from Liz Jackman saying, 'Bruno has been found!'

Sarah jumped in her car and went to this property thinking she was going to pick Bruno up and take him home to Emma. When she got there, she burst into tears. It wasn't Bruno. This dog was too old. I'd just jumped in my car to go up there myself when I got another message from Liz saying, 'It's not him.'

We all went from this huge high to this crushing low. Sarah was hysterical, but she knew she needed to take this dog to Emma and show her that it wasn't Bruno. She took him and Emma walked out and saw the dog in the car. She gave him a kiss on the head and said to Sarah, 'It's okay, darling, but please take him to the vet because he needs help.'

I came home and thought, *I need to sit out the front of my house and cry my eyes out. I need to talk to Emma on the phone and figure out where we go from here.* I was hysterical. I'd held it together all this time and I was saying to Emma, 'I don't know what to do.'

Emma is very dear to me. I'm not just her dog's trainer. She's not just a girl and her dog – she's one of my very dear friends. I share my clients' lives, we are like family. It's been my life's greatest joy to be part of the Whiskey's Wish program. Working with people like Emma – veterans and frontline people – and watching the difference those dogs can make is just amazing.

All we could do was keep praying that Bruno was going to come home. We just had to hope he was sitting somewhere, waiting for that water to go down so he could get home.

Emma Broe

By day two, I knew had to get into SES mode. I knew Liz and Linda had put up posts on their Facebook pages, but I switched off from everybody. Apparently I spoke to my psychologist, but I have no memory of that conversation. I didn't dare talk to anyone because I couldn't hear the name Bruno. I couldn't cope. I would have fallen apart.

When you're looking for a child, you can't think of the emotional side otherwise you won't cope.

I'd already walked kilometres, done a typical land search. I would feed Arya and Mooch at 6 a.m., play with them, and then head off for my first search. I did that three or four times a day, going out for the last time at midnight. I was doing twenty hours of walking per day and it wasn't easy terrain. It was a four-wheel drive track, very steep and rocky.

Unbeknown to me, this big media machine was going on in the background. Sarah was drawing up posters.

I was told there had been a sighting at Davies Creek Mountain Bike Park, that Bruno was somewhere out there socialising with another dog. Sarah and I raced up there and started doing the rounds, talking to bush-walkers and mountain bikers.

Three local police stations were informed. Three weeks before Bruno vanished, a Queensland Police dog, PD Quizz, had gone missing near Brisbane. Because I'm a first responder and Bruno is a service dog, we're like one of their own. They treated it with real importance, which was lovely.

The rain stopped on the fourth day, but the creek was still raging. I was getting to the point where I felt I was running out of options. My mind got very bleak. I went up to Davies Creek Falls and climbed over the safety fence. I thought, *I can't do this anymore.*

But I stopped to think, and I thought of Scott Jackman. I thought of how he lost Whiskey to inopera-ble cancer after just a year with him. I realised that if I gave up, I'd be letting Bruno down, but I'd also be letting down Scott and Whiskey's Wish. If Scott was strong enough to lose Whiskey and move on with his life and start Whiskey's Wish, I knew had to bring Bruno home, dead or alive.

A week after he disappeared, I got a call saying, 'Sarah's on the way, we've found him!' I knew in my head, *No, you haven't.* I carried on preparing my pack for the day, because I knew I was going out to search.

Sarah arrived and I knew it wasn't Bruno. I walked down with a mug of coffee in my hand.

She stopped the car at the gate and she was crying, saying, 'Is it him? Is it him?'

Before I got to the back seat I said, 'No, darling.'

He was a German shepherd with a black collar, but he was very old and very grey, blind in one eye. He was very lovely, but he wasn't Bruno. I gave him the biggest hug and whispered to him that we would find his mum. I thought, *If nothing else comes out of this, at least he'll find his mum.* It turned out he was from NSW and was able to be reunited with his family.

I waited for Sarah to get back on the highway and then I set off. I picked up my SES backpack, which holds all my land search equipment and resources. I had rope, a first aid kit, carabiners and dog treats in a little ziplock bag. I put a flask of water in one side and a flask of coffee in the other side. I rolled a couple of cigarettes and took my wallet.

My idea was that I was going to throw the rope across the creek and hope to god that it wrapped itself around something so I could pull it taught and use it to pull myself across. Incredibly, it did – first time in my life! I had a gut feeling Bruno was over there. I just had to get to him.

I put a foot in the water and *whoosh* – I was gone. I got swept 200 metres downstream. My heartbeat was going like mad, but I thought, *Bugger this*. I've got a 'f— you' attitude when life is really shitty.

I was in the middle of this raging creek. What lay ahead of me was masses and masses of deep, dense, rocky bush. I managed to grab a log and haul myself up. Earlier in the year I'd fallen over and snapped my wrist really badly; I had no strength in it, so I didn't have my left hand to rely on. I thought, *Knowing me, I'll break my wrist again.* It was bloody painful.

I was halfway across and could just see the bank ahead of me. But then I hit a submerged rock and my legs went out from underneath me. The current was so strong and I was exhausted. I couldn't hold on to the log. I just let go. The speed at which I was swept away was like a luge.

I was bouncing off rocks and logs, underwater the whole time. I had a big stick that I was using as a sort of pointer and I was propelling myself away from clusters of rock with it.

It must have only taken seconds, but I went on this mad mental ride. There were so many thoughts that just rushed into my head all in one go. First I was thinking, *I was going to take my life, and now that I've got this plan to find Bruno I'm going to die – I can't die now!* My next thought was that I couldn't be someone that a first responder from the SES was going to find.

Then I thought, *I'm going to survive, but my coffee and my cigarettes are going to be gone – that'd be right.*

Suddenly I came to a stop near some fallen trees. My chest felt like it was going to explode. I was literally looking up from under the water and I thought, *Shit, I'm alive.*

I'd gone 790 metres – way past the neighbour's house. My coffee and my cigarettes were still there, but I was hurting so badly. I've got arthritis and I've had a broken back and neck, so I've got metal in my back.

I sat down and it kind of hit me a bit hard. I thought I'd lost my boy, and I was hurting. I sat there and I continued to call him for about ten or fifteen minutes. I'd promised myself he was on that track. I thought I'd be heading up the track, and he'd be coming towards me, and we'd head home together.

I limped my way back home. I found leeches and paralysis ticks in places you'd never want to find them.

I was on the phone to Linda when Arya and Mooch started barking. Actually, they were shrieking. I've never heard anything like it. I said, 'I've got to go,' and around the corner comes this very happy looking, very skinny and very wet German shepherd.

Linda Mair

When I heard Emma's other dogs start barking and she went silent on the phone, my first thought was that someone had come down her driveway with a dead dog. She said, 'I've got to go, I'll call you back,' and hung up.

A few seconds later she sent me a photo of Bruno lying, exhausted, on the back verandah of her house. He had come up the back, from the creek, soaking wet.

It was just an amazing moment. My wish for a miracle was granted.

What I believe happened is that when Emma was washed down that creek not two hours earlier, she was screaming Bruno's name, and I think he heard her and made one last effort to come home.

I've had pets all my life. I've had horses since I was seven. I was a council animal control officer. I started working with Whiskey's Wish in 2017, but I've been working with dogs for thirty years. I've heard some amazing stories, but this will go down as one of the most amazing. Even now it still makes me tear up.

I can explain a lot of behavioural stuff because I've had that training, but there are also miraculous things that dogs do. This is a story of why you don't ever lose faith. Liz held us together even in the lowest of lows. She just kept saying, 'I believe in miracles. He will come home – don't give up.'

It's beyond belief how Emma did what she did, and testament to the strength of human character. She's so unwell there are times she can't walk, yet she had been putting that pack on her back for seven days and traipsing through the bush. She went into that raging creek and roped it all up, but just couldn't hold on.

Any of us that has a pet really has a service animal – it's just not necessarily wearing the jacket. At some stage they all do something of benefit for their owners. But these service dogs really do help the owners get up and face each day. They do most of their work at home. What Bruno does for Emma during her darkest times at home is not trained by us. They just know.

Emma Broe

Bruno came home from the exact direction of the route I'd taken, where I'd felt so sure he would be. He must have come over the logs that had fallen, picked up my scent where I'd sat and had coffee, and followed me home.

I went to my knees – and then I saw the blood everywhere. There was nothing wrong with him except that his feet were ripped raw. I think it was from being in the creek and trying to grab onto something. I immediately bathed his legs and checked him for ticks. He drank so much water and then just sort of sank down because he was so tired.

In the afternoon we were taken to the vet by a friend. I got him out of the car and my friend said, 'Don't look now' – because she knew I was in a very bad way mentally – 'but there's about twenty people looking at you.'

Suddenly this woman starts running towards me and stops with her hand over her mouth and says, 'Please tell me this is *the* Bruno.' I said yes and she turned around and said to the other people, who didn't know each other, 'It's him!'

The vet nurse came out saying, 'Is it really him? Is it Bruno from the radio and the TV?' They checked him over and said he was absolutely fine. I didn't look at the vet bill until I got home – they had charged me for a short consult for a miniature breed, and the antibiotics were zero dollars.

When he came home he was a baby again. He needed his mum.

Strangers still stop me in the street. People will stand there and stare. Eventually they pluck up the courage to come up and say, 'Is that Bruno?' He gathers a crowd everywhere we go. We get strangers taking photos of him. He is a dog that people gravitate to.

Even to this day, I really haven't sat down with Linda and talked about it. I was in my own world, but it sounds like behind the scenes it was like a military operation. I couldn't go on Facebook because I would get emotional if I even saw his name. I was focused on the grid search because it was the only thing I could do.

I wanted to give Linda and Sarah a present. Nothing I could give them was going to repay them, but I had to think of something. I remembered the reasons why I chose not to give everything up, and all the love and support they were giving me, so I carved a heart out of white cedar and carved a pawprint into it. I wrote in the card, *Forever imprinted on your heart*. The love they gave me, and the legacy of Whiskey, gave me the strength to carry on and keep looking for my boy.

People don't understand what dogs are capable of doing. These assistance dogs are not just dogs. Bruno is not just a dog. Whiskey's Wish has opened up my life, but without Bruno I wouldn't have gone to Whiskey's Wish. I wouldn't be here now without him.

Buddy

The legal beagle

If there is one thing dogs excel at it's, well, simply being dogs.

They are inexhaustible play machines. They possess finely tuned treat-seeking systems, also known as noses. They're very good at sneaking into forbidden napping spots, such as the sofa and their humans' beds. And, of course, they have a special knack for getting into all sorts of adorable scrapes.

Dogs are naturals at living life to the fullest, loving intensely, and wringing every available bit of joy out of every single moment. It's this inherent joie de vivre that once prompted the late comedian Gilda Radner to quip, 'I think dogs are the most amazing creatures; they give unconditional love. For me, they are the role model for being alive.'

At least, the above is true of *most* dogs – but not all.

Some dogs live the majority of their lives without ever having the opportunity to play, lick, dig or love. They don't get the chance to develop their innate *dogness*. Is there anything sadder than a canine that just doesn't know how to dog?

This is often the reality for dogs that are used in scientific research. Cosmetic testing on animals is banned in Australia but medical research still uses dogs, cats and other animals, including mice, guinea pigs, rabbits, hamsters, ferrets, birds, fish, reptiles, native animals, and even exotic species such as baboons.

Frustratingly little is known about how many animals are held by research facilities in Australia, because it is an industry shrouded in secrecy. There is currently no federal law requiring facilities to disclose those facts and figures. In 2017, Humane Research Australia estimated that there were as many as 11,369 dogs and 2587 cats used in research around the nation, but nobody knows for sure how many are being used for experimentation.

Shockingly, research facilities are also not required to re-home animals that have outlived their usefulness as research subjects, nor do they have to reveal what becomes of them. People who want to adopt former research animals, generally speaking, can't. These research facilities can essentially do anything they like with animals that have been used for science for years at a time and never say a word about it.

It is a situation that is quite simply unacceptable to Animal Justice Party (AJP) MP Emma Hurst, a Member of the Legislative Council in New South Wales. Emma has been fighting for animals used in medical research since long before she was elected to state parliament. She used to run a rescue specifically for animals that had been used in medical experimentation, finding new homes for the few guinea pigs, mice and even goats she could liberate from research facilities. She would have rescued dogs and cats, too, but she couldn't get access to them.

When she pushed to be able to rehome more animals, Emma says she was told by people working in the field that the preference was to euthanise rather than release them, to avoid drawing attention to the fact that live experimentation still happens.

'I believe that many research facilities that use cats and dogs are refusing to release these animals because they are concerned about public backlash. Current laws allow for healthy animals to be killed at the end of experimentation,' Emma explains. 'After everything these animals have endured, euthanasia is incomprehensible. The killing of healthy animals to avoid public scrutiny is never the answer. If there is nothing to hide then there should be no need for the secrecy.'

In Australia, only New South Wales has implemented mandatory reporting for the state's research centres, thanks in large part to the AJP. Since 2019, institutions have been required to report on the dogs and cats used in their medical research.

In 2020, 884 cats and 2553 dogs were used for medical experimentation in New South Wales. The state government reported that, in 2019, only thirty dogs used in research were re-homed. In 2020, none were rehomed.

'This means these animals will have their bodies recycled through various experiments. There is no legislation that caps the number of years an animal can be forced to endure repeat experiments. Animals could remain in research facilities their entire lives,' says Emma.

She says many people are unaware that taxpayer money is likely used to fund the continued breeding and use of animals in experimentation. That's because, again, research institutions are not required to divulge how much of the public money they receive is funnelled into the practice. 'The government refuses to say exactly how much money is given to this industry, and there is no transparency about the types of experiments taxpayers are funding.'

In the United States, some states have passed 'right to release' laws that require research animals to be released to rescue groups rather than be euthanised. The AJP proposed similar legislation in NSW in 2018, before Emma was in parliament, but the bill was opposed by the government.

'The rejection of the bill leaves animals who have already endured having their bodies recycled through experiments facing death row,' she says. 'I can't stop thinking about the animals that will be born into animal experimentation – and die there.'

The AJP supports government funding for alternatives to the use of animals in experimentation, and Emma and her party share a desire to see the animals involved in medical research being given a second chance at life.

'Most of us consider cats and dogs to be members of the family, yet thousands are still used for medical experimentation in Australia today. Current laws allow for healthy animals to be killed at the end of experimentation. It's time to change those laws.'

That's why Emma and the AJP are now developing a new piece of legislation, one that will require mandatory rehoming for animals released from experimentation as well as work to defund taxpayer-funded animal experiments.

The proposed legislation is called Buddy's Law, and its inspiration is a senior dog who is living proof that release from a research facility can be just the beginning of an incredible new life.

It is impossible to spend more than five minutes in the company of Patrice Pandeleos without being swept up by her passion for animals. Her love of all creatures great and small is well known by everyone, from her family, friends and colleagues to the café staff and boutique owners in the inner-city Sydney suburb she calls home.

Just as renowned is Patrice's devotion to her canine sidekick, Buddy.

'Buddy loves being out and about. I take him everywhere, even shopping. He knows the shops I go into, so he'll drag me in there and just lie on the floor,' she says with a laugh. 'A lot of the shops I go to regularly have bought a packet of dog treats just for Buddy. I'll take him to the pub on a Sunday afternoon and the staff will give him his own doggy Sunday roast.'

Patrice has had a penchant for collecting animals in need for as long as she can remember. When she was just five or six years old, she launched a clandestine mission to brighten the life of a neighbour's dog, who she felt wasn't receiving enough attention.

Ben, a sweet-natured Rottweiler whose 60-kilogram frame dwarfed the young Patrice, spent his days chained and alone in a suburban backyard.

'I would sneak into the yard every day, let him off his chain and take him for a walk. I thought the neighbours didn't notice, until one day they said, "We see that you're doing this and you don't have to sneak – you can just come in,"' she says. 'Ben was my dog after that.'

Growing up, she rescued countless dogs and cats, and also had three horses, which were agisted on a property south of Sydney.

'Even as a little kid I would find stray animals and take

them home. I always had dog and cat food stashed at home in case I found an animal, which drove my parents nuts. Over the years I've had rats, mice, crabs and probably more than thirty birds. I even had a three-legged turtle that I found in the gutter of a suburban street,' she says. 'I think some people just love animals. We're born that way! Everyone who knows me knows that my number one interest in life is animals. You do get branded "that person" in your circle. It's a running joke. But I can't imagine my life without an animal in it. It's not even a question.'

As well as being ever-prepared to assist waifs and strays, Patrice also has a long history of volunteering with animal welfare organisations. She has worked with orang-utans and sun bears in Borneo, wildlife in Africa, the Sydney Dogs and Cats Home, and during a stint living in Western Australia was a regular volunteer at Perth's Dogs' Refuge Home. She also served on the board of directors of the charity Coalition for Conservation and has twice run for the NSW Parliament.

All of it, she says, was vital preparation for meeting the animal that would change her life in more ways than she could ever have imagined.

In June 2019, Patrice, who is the owner and managing director of a communications agency, was on a press-familiarisation trip with a group of journalists in the island nation of Malta. During that trip, she spotted an intriguing post on Emma Hurst's Facebook page. The post detailed Emma and the AJP's efforts to pass the 'right to release' legislation in the NSW Parliament that would make it mandatory for animals used in medical research to be released at the end of experimentation.

Patrice had been following Emma's social media accounts for some time and had been stunned to discover the extent of medical research on animals in Australia. 'I knew we didn't use animals for cosmetic testing in Australia, so I was shocked to learn we're still using dogs and cats for medical research. I get that there are times when we might need to use an animal for research – I am realistic about that. If you said to someone, "Doing this research might save kids from dying of cancer," I think most people would understand. But there's zero transparency. Medical researchers are still putting animals in isolation, with no stimulation, for long periods of time. There needs to be a high level of transparency over what people are doing and how much money is going towards it.'

In her Facebook post, Emma shared the story of an adorable beagle–kelpie mix she called Max – a medical research dog who was one of the first to be made available for rehoming. After enduring eight years of undisclosed experiments, he was now in search of a kind and patient forever home.

Max wasn't the dog's real name – Emma couldn't reveal that. Nor could she say which research facility he'd come from or what sort of testing he'd been subjected to.

Kimmy's trainer always knew her working dog was special, but she was blown away when the kelpie sold for $27,000 at the famous Casterton Kelpie Muster.

(Kahlee O'Leary; Ashley Meaburn)

In the middle of a helicopter rescue during the catastrophic Northern Rivers floods, DJ fell into the floodwater. When his owners found him several days later, literally clinging on to life, they became believers in miracles. *(Mark O'Toole)*

Sally the sweet senior Staffy was the apple of Karen and Jamie Goullet's eye – so much so that the couple started a dog sanctuary in her honour. Inspired by Sally, they've given a loving home to dozens of senior dogs and dogs in need of palliative care. *(Karen Goullett)*

A peaceful evening stroll turned into a dramatic rescue when Basil the Rottweiler plucked a drowning child from Canberra's Lake Burley Griffin. *(Terry Cunningham)*

Cam Zschech thought his family might get a laugh from a video of Lexi the Jack Russell terrier 'driving' his ute – he didn't expect her to become the feel-good story of the year.

(Cam Zschech)

Bruno the psychiatric support dog saves Emma Broe's life every day. So when he went missing in a creek on Australia Day 2022, she called on all her skills as an SES volunteer to find him, ultimately risking her own life to save his. *(Emma Broe)*

Buddy the beagle spent the first eight years of his life in a cage, being used for medical research. Now that he's found a true home, he's the spokespooch for new laws that will help other animals used for medical testing. *(Patrice Pandeleos)*

Rescue pup Chelsea wasn't trained as a diabetes alert dog – but that didn't matter to her the night she instinctively saved her owner from slipping into a diabetic coma.

(Steph Walters)

After being rescued from appalling neglect, Billy the terrier found his best life. His story of recovery, transforming into a beloved family companion, saw him declared a 'hero dog' and chosen as an RSPCA Million Paws Walk ambassador.

(Lisa Weber)

After being rescued from a chained-up and malnourished life, not only was Grover the border collie nursed back to health by Claire Garth, he became the inspiration for her children's book series. *(Claire Garth)*

She never had puppies of her own, but that didn't stop 'Mumma Zura' the American Staffordshire terrier from becoming the doting 'mum' to more than 200 foster puppies.

(Caroline Zambrano; Scott Banning)

All dogs love walkies, but Frankie took it to the extreme when he walked more than 4000 kilometres from Sydney to Darwin to help his owner, Benny Scott, conquer drug addiction.
(Benny Scott)

2022

MY FIRST SCHOOL PHOTO

Returning to school after months of online learning during the pandemic was always going to be tricky for some children, so Sydney's Trinity Catholic Primary School employed a new staff member to make things easier: Yale the wellbeing dog. *(Cathy Hey)*

When COVID-19 meant that St Vincent's Hospital Melbourne's volunteer dog teams could no longer visit patients, staffer Judy Clover brought Macca along for the job – the Yorkshire terrier was such a hit, he was honoured with a special award. *(Judy Clover)*

I've spent the majority of my adult life with Tex (rear) and Delilah, the Nova Scotia Duck Tolling Retrievers. They taught me that all dogs are amazing, whether they're saving lives or simply cuddling their owners on the couch. *(Laura Greaves)*

'My three-legged cat, Princess Audrey, who I'd had for sixteen years, had died three months earlier. I was so heartbroken that I couldn't even look in the direction of another cat. I wasn't going to adopt another animal for a while because I was too upset,' Patrice recalls. 'Emma said in her post, "If you can give him a home, apply here." I read Max's story and found myself saying to the two journalists I was with in Malta, "Look at this dog, I have to apply for him."'

She did just that, emailing her application from her hotel room. The response from the unnamed rescue group looking after Max was swift. Before she knew it, Patrice was setting her alarm for a video interview at four o'clock in the morning Maltese time.

'I had my first interview with his people from Malta. I flew back into Sydney at nine o'clock the next morning, and Max arrived at my house for his meet 'n' greet at midday.'

Max, it turned out, was really called Buddy – and Patrice was instantly smitten. She describes him as 'the height and shape of a kelpie but with a beagle face'. The moment Buddy set paw inside her front door, she knew that the handsome eight-year-old was home for good. 'Buddy was my first dog on my own, and he was just an angel from day one.'

Not everyone was convinced that adopting him was a wise decision, however.

'People were saying, "Are you sure? He's lived in a cage for eight years. He's never walked outside or lived in a house. He'll destroy your home,"' Patrice recalls. 'But I was just saying, "I'm single, I love animals and I've always wanted a rescue dog – if anyone has the time and patience to work through all that, it's me."'

But the pessimists weren't entirely wrong. Buddy was indeed thought to have lived in a cage for the entirety of his eight years. He was a senior dog who had never experienced things even most puppies are familiar with. He had never seen tiled or wooden floors. Treats were baffling. He couldn't walk upstairs. He'd never even been outside before being taken in by the rescue group. And, saddest of all, Buddy had no idea how to play.

The first thing Patrice did after touching down in Sydney on the morning of Buddy's arrival was race to the nearest pet shop. She bought as many treats and toys as she could carry, then laid them all out on the floor for him to inspect.

'I had probably twenty toys and twenty bags of treats all laid out, and he just didn't understand what they were. He had obviously never seen a toy before. He was very timid and nervous. I threw a ball for him and he ran and hid,' she says.

'I was so excited to see his reactions to all these new things, and seeing that he was so scared and just didn't understand what they were was hard. Everything was new and a bit of a shock for him. I can't imagine a dog never having access to all of that.'

As well as being thoroughly confused, Buddy was also

very thin and his coat was dull, both indications of malnutrition.

Patrice was required to sign a non-disclosure agreement in order to adopt Buddy, which meant she would never be permitted to know where he had come from or the nature of the experiments conducted on him. She has her suspicions, however.

'He doesn't have major scars or anything like that, but both his ears are full of haematomas [blood-filled pockets inside the ear flaps],' she says. 'They'd absolutely been injecting his ears a lot, though I have no idea what with. I'll never know exactly what happened to Buddy or what he was put through, and I think that's a sad thing. I'll always want to know, because then I could shout it from the rooftops to stop it happening to other dogs.'

Buddy weighed around 18 kilograms when he came to Patrice, and within a month was tipping the scales at 22 kilograms. His coat improved to being so shiny that Patrice's groomer advised her not to wash him so often.

He was a little jittery on walks to begin with. 'If we were walking down the street and someone pulled out their phone quickly, he would hit the ground like a bomb had gone off,' says Patrice.

But before too long he was friends with everyone at the dog park. 'We walk to Centennial Park most days and it didn't take very long at all before he knew the way and would drag me there because he was so excited. The first month that I got him I lost three kilos from all the walking, and he put on three kilos from all the treats.' she says. 'At first I thought I'd walk him a lot to wear him out, because he's part kelpie and needs exercise, but I realised I was just making him fitter and wearing myself out.'

Buddy's affinity for other creatures, whether they be dogs, cats or humans, was something of a surprise to Patrice, given that he had spent so much of his life deprived of company. It would have made sense if he'd been reactive towards other dogs, or shy around humans, but that simply wasn't the case.

'Buddy's nickname is "The Dogfather", because the other dogs at the dog park think he's the boss. When he enters the park they all run over and lick his face. He's the only one they don't crash tackle to the ground.'

Patrice also started taking Buddy to work every day, helping him to come further out of his shell. He received a steady stream of pats and cuddles from staff, who also taught him to high-five. At almost nine years old, he had learned his first party trick.

'He became really well socialised really quickly. I thought it would take a lot longer because he was an older dog, but within six months he was what most people would consider to be a normal dog,' says Patrice. 'There's that saying, "You can't teach an old dog new tricks," but Buddy is the opposite of that. He's a bit like Peter Pan. It was almost like having a puppy, in a way, because he was seeing everything for the first time. He's just a great dog.'

In just a short time, Buddy became a poster dog for what is possible for released research animals. His transformation from sad and frightened test subject to happy and beloved pet was so remarkable that Buddy soon found himself making headlines.

Emma Hurst and Buddy began their new lives at precisely the same time. On the same day that Buddy was released from a medical research facility into the care of a rescue group, Emma was making her inaugural speech in the NSW Parliament.

A registered psychologist who had worked for many years in media, animal advocacy and political lobbying with not-for-profit organisations, Emma swapped the private sector for the public service when she was elected to the Legislative Council in March 2019. But while Emma had been the conduit between the rescue group caring for Buddy and his new owner, Patrice, she didn't actually meet the brave beagle until after he was settled in his forever home.

When she saw how beautifully he had adapted to his post-research life, Emma knew Buddy would be the perfect spokespooch for the AJP's revamped 'right to release' bill, following the government's opposition to a similar bill in 2018.

Emma met with Patrice and Buddy for a puppuccino and asked Patrice how she would feel about the legislation being named after her sweet dog.

'Meeting Buddy, you wouldn't know he was a survivor of medical experimentation. I don't know what was done to him. Most people don't. In fact, he is one of the very few who have made it out alive,' Emma says. 'He might seem like a regular dog when you meet him at the café, but when you speak to Patrice about her early experiences with Buddy you find out that he didn't know what a lead was or how to go for "walkies". At eight years of age, he had to learn the very basic, everyday dog things. Buddy has the same big heart as any dog, and yet he didn't get the same chances in life – until now. He should have known what grass felt like under his paws. He should have met other dogs like him in parks, and snuggled on cold nights with a doting human who loved him. This is what every dog deserves.'

Patrice didn't have to think twice about Emma's offer; she immediately accepted the invitation for Buddy to front the campaign.

'I said, "Yes, I think it's a great idea." I think Emma is a great campaigner for animals. Buddy is one of the lucky ones. He donated his body to research and he – and dogs like him – deserve more. Although I do feel like Buddy has achieved more in life than I have,' she says with a chuckle. 'How is it possible that I've run for election twice and now he is the one that has a bill in parliament?'

*

While Emma and the AJP's championing of the bill continued, with Buddy as the furry face of the campaign, Patrice wanted to make up for lost time. When Buddy first came to her, she let him experience all the things he missed out on during his years as a test subject, deciding not to impose any rules on him – a strategy she now admits has somewhat backfired (albeit with very cute results).

'It was great for the first two years, but now he thinks he's the boss of me. He's learned some bad habits. One of his best friends is a beagle–pug mix called Flo, who walks around and barks at everyone for treats. It doesn't matter if she doesn't know them, she'll still try her luck. Now Buddy does that too. It's translated to him walking into the local coffee shop every morning and barking for treats.'

(It was in this same café, incidentally, where Patrice found herself telling a stranger all about Buddy. That man, who had never owned a dog before, was so moved that he promptly went and adopted a dog from the same rescue organisation.)

But even Buddy's occasionally cheeky behaviour is a source of delight for Patrice, who marvels daily at just how far he has come. His company was a boon during Sydney's COVID-19 lockdowns in 2020 and 2021.

'It was so amazing to have a dog during the pandemic. I was living alone and working from home, and if I hadn't had Buddy I feel like I never would have left the house or got any fresh air,' she says. 'We'd all take our dogs to the park every day and it was just that little bit of socialisation that kept everyone sane. In the area where I live, I know more than a hundred people now, just through Buddy. Dogs are such amazing icebreakers.'

The same naysayers who had cautioned Patrice against adopting Buddy also warned that their time together might be short-lived due to his senior status, but he is now eleven years old and has the energy and enthusiasm of a much younger dog.

He was at risk of developing arthritis due to his age and the years spent confined to a cramped cage, but his 10-kilometre daily walks with Patrice have helped keep him limber. He also takes supplements to support his joints and Patrice cooks hot meals for him every day. None of it is too much trouble, she says.

In June 2022, Buddy's Law passed the upper house of the NSW Parliament. To become law, it still needs to pass the lower house as well. When it does, the thousands of dogs and cats used for medical research in the state will have the opportunity to live the rest of their lives in loving homes – just like Buddy.

Rescue dogs are often stigmatised, unfairly labelled as 'damaged' when the mistreatment they suffered was not their fault, and can be overcome with kindness and time. When – not if – Buddy's Law is passed, Emma is confident that people will be willing to take a chance on a former research dog.

'Dogs have an amazing ability to forgive and see the best in humans, even when perhaps we don't deserve it. If we can't give dogs like Buddy a second chance at life then humanity is all but lost,' she says. 'I think many Australians, being the animal lovers that we are, would be willing to open their home to a dog like Buddy – to give them a chance to really experience life and love. These animals need our voices and they need our protection.'

But she is pragmatic about the fact that many dogs like Buddy will need very special owners. 'Some of these animals will need a patient family. They do have special needs and it is important that anyone taking an ex-research animal is aware of this and can give the animal time to adjust,' says Emma. 'But so many dogs like Buddy *do* adjust. Seeing Buddy live his best life reminds me what we are fighting for: to give every animal the chance they so truly deserve.'

Patrice wholeheartedly agrees. For her, the ordeal research animals have been put through is exactly what makes them so deserving of a beautiful existence when they are finally free. Buddy had no choice in what was done to him for eight years. We owe him, and all animals like him, a debt we can never fully repay.

'You have to make sure that your pet has the best living situation. If you take a dog like Buddy, you have an extra responsibility to give him a special life,' Patrice says.

'Dogs like him do something for the greater good and there should be a point where that stops and they get an exceptional life after that.'

And that's what it comes down to in the end: amazing dogs deserve amazing lives.

Chelsea

The life-saving terrier

There are very few dog owners out there that truly have no expectations of their pet. *Low* expectations, sure. Walk nicely on the lead. Provide cuddles on demand. Pee outside, not on the carpet. Don't bite the postman. The basics. It's not asking a lot, but it's still asking for something.

At the other end of the spectrum are the owners and handlers that expect the world from their four-legged friends. Sniff out the contraband! Conquer the agility course faster than all the other dogs! Locate the person within the collapsed building! High standards indeed.

But one of the great things about dogs is that, whether our expectations of them are sky high or rock bottom, they always manage to go above and beyond. They're forever finding ways to do more than we asked for. They love to surprise us – sometimes in ways we'd rather they didn't, as anyone who's ever discovered their favourite shoes chewed to bits or the contents of their rubbish bin spread all over the kitchen floor will attest.

Often, however, dogs will exceed our expectations in truly astounding ways. They will do something we never dreamed them capable of – something we can never adequately thank them for.

Like saving a life.

Lifelong dog owner Steph Walters has never demanded much more from her canine companions than love, loyalty and, as she's grown up and become a keen marathon runner, a willing occasional partner for her training runs.

'I'm actually allergic to dogs – I get a really itchy nose around them – but I've always loved them,' she confesses. 'My family had a golden retriever, Mitsy, when I was in primary school. Then we got a Cavalier King Charles spaniel called Lucy in 2003, when I was in Year Ten. Lucy was so lovely. We used to walk her every afternoon with our friend who had a Beagle called Rocky.'

For Steph, an itchy nose was a small price to pay for the constant calming presence of a dog, because there were times growing up when life was anything but calm. In June 1993, when she was five years old, Steph experienced a health emergency that changed the course of her life. She had recently recovered from one of those run-of-the-mill viruses that young children are so susceptible to. She was back at school, but something wasn't quite right. Steph seemed to be constantly running to the toilet – and on a couple of occasions she didn't make it in time.

'I wet myself at school a couple of times and my mum thought, *I'd better take her to the doctor*,' she recalls.

Steph's GP decided to conduct a simple finger prick test to check her blood glucose levels, as high blood sugar can be a cause of excessive urination. The doctor was shocked by the test result.

'He realised my levels were high and told Mum I should go straight to emergency. I remember Mum calling up to Dad on the balcony of the unit we lived in, saying, "We've got to go to the hospital!"'

Further testing in hospital led to a confronting diagnosis: Steph had type-1 diabetes.

One of the most common chronic childhood conditions, type-1 diabetes is an autoimmune condition that occurs when the pancreas stops producing insulin because the cells that make it have been destroyed by the body's own immune system. The exact cause of type-1 diabetes remains unknown, but there is thought to be a genetic link and the onset is usually triggered by an environmental factor, such as the virus Steph had contracted. There is no cure, and unlike type-2 diabetes it cannot be prevented with lifestyle changes, although careful dietary management is still necessary.

People with the condition depend on daily insulin, delivered via injections or an insulin pump, and they must test their blood glucose levels multiple times every day.

'The technology and diagnostics weren't as good back then. There were no insulin pumps – it was all injections,' Steph says. An insulin pump attaches to the body, requiring only one needle-prick, and then supplies a constant flow of insulin, whereas Steph had to receive regular injections to keep her levels in check. 'I don't remember ever being scared, but obviously for my parents it was a big shock. Having to inject your child would be pretty scary.'

Steph's emergency dash to hospital turned into a ten-day stay, which was understandably not much fun.

'I guess I didn't really understand at that point what my diagnosis would mean for my life. What I remember from that time are things like being given a bowl of peas for dinner in hospital and being really upset!'

She also remembers the distress she felt at being apart from her identical twin sister, Melissa, for the first time in their young lives. 'That was really tough. I remember one time looking in the mirror and thinking it was Mel and feeling so sad when I realised it was my own reflection.'

The identical twin sibling of a child with type-1 diabetes has a high chance of developing the condition, and that's exactly what happened in Mel's case – though Mel didn't receive her diagnosis until she was nineteen.

Steph recalls being more upset about her sister's diagnosis than her own. 'I'd lived with diabetes almost my whole life by that stage, and I think it was easier for me to cope with because the diagnosis came early. When Mel was diagnosed I was so upset, because I knew what she would have to go through,' she says.

One of the things she grieved on her sister's behalf was the inevitable end of her carefree attitude to food and nutrition. People with type-1 diabetes must carefully monitor everything they eat and drink to ensure they administer enough insulin to compensate for the carbohydrates they consume, which are turned into glucose in the blood.

It can be exhausting performing the necessary mental arithmetic before every meal or snack, says Steph. 'Apparently type-1 diabetics make an additional 180 health decisions per day. Practically every five minutes I'm having to make another decision. Even if I just eat something small, I have to think about how many carbs are in it. Most of the time I can just work it out, and my insulin pump is great because it works out how much insulin I need, but sometimes I have to google it.'

With this extra layer of complexity to almost everything she does, it's really no wonder Steph has always enjoyed the uncomplicated company of dogs.

Tragically, the family dog Lucy died from a suspected spider bite when she was just six years old. By then, Steph had already moved out of the family home in the southwestern Sydney suburb of Wattle Grove, relocating to the regional city of Wagga Wagga to attend university. Though she was enjoying life in her new town, Steph found herself really missing canine companionship.

There was only one thing for it: a visit to the local council's animal shelter. There she fell head-over-heels in love with a young corgi-mix. She named him Darcy, after the hero of Jane Austen's classic *Pride and Prejudice*; it's one of Steph's favourite books. He also had a middle name, Staples, after her favourite author CS (Clive Staples) Lewis.

Two years later, in 2010, Steph visited a shelter in south-west Sydney to adopt a friend for him. This time she left with a mixed-breed terrier puppy called Chelsea, named for the English Premier League team Steph supports. Chelsea's middle name is Liv, after Liverpool Football Club.

Together, Steph, Darcy and Chelsea were an inseparable trio. Well, except for a brief but agonising period in March 2014 when they were separated against their will.

Steph had completed her Bachelor of Arts degree and, while she settled into her new job in marketing and re-established herself in Sydney, she'd temporarily moved back in with her parents. One night, while she was out for a run with both dogs, Darcy vanished.

'It was late at night and Darcy came off his lead and ran off. We were two or three kilometres from home. I have really bad night vision, so I couldn't see which way he went,' she explains.

She was frantic, searching high and low for her beloved pooch. She plastered her neighbourhood with 'lost dog' posters and, thanks to the support of a lost pets Facebook group for her area, search parties comprised of kind-hearted strangers regularly canvassed the local streets.

And yet days passed with no sign of Darcy. Steph was starting to worry she might never find her sweet boy, and Chelsea was lost without her playmate. 'Darcy and Chelsea always got along really well. When Darcy was missing, Chelsea was the most miserable I've ever seen her. She was just lying around, not wanting to do anything.'

After ten long days, an antsy Steph decided to go for another late-night run. She needed to burn off some of the anxiety she was feeling as a result of having no clue as to Darcy's whereabouts.

'I was running right near my house, going past a side street, and this lady came walking out of her house with Darcy. I was like, "That's my dog!"'

Darcy was overjoyed to see his rightful owner, covering Steph's face with enthusiastic doggy kisses.

'She had stolen him – that's why she was walking him at night,' explains Steph.

She was so thrilled to be reunited with the dog she'd feared she might never see again that she didn't think to take the woman to task over the blatant dognapping. 'She said she'd just found him and was going to take him to the vet the next day, but she had put a brand new collar on him. Where I found him was only five hundred metres from my house, so he'd obviously been making his way home when she took him. But I was so excited to actually find my dog again that I just ran straight home.'

If she hadn't decided to go for a run that night, if she hadn't glanced down that side street, and if the woman that stole Darcy hadn't been sneaking out for a clandestine walk under the cover of darkness at that very moment, Steph and Darcy could well have been separated forever. The sequence of events that had to unfold in order for them to find each other is nothing short of amazing.

But Darcy isn't the real subject of this amazing dog story.

That story is about Chelsea, and what she did next.

Having lived with type-1 diabetes for almost thirty years, managing the condition is second nature to Steph – but sometimes even she gets caught out by insulin miscalculations or uncooperative blood glucose levels.

Without insulin, the body cannot turn glucose (sugar) into energy, and it burns its own fats instead. This process releases chemical substances called ketones into the blood, which can accumulate to life threatening levels, causing hyperglycaemia or ketoacidosis. Untreated ketoacidosis can lead to death – this is what sent five-year-old Steph to hospital.

When blood glucose levels (BGLs) are too *low*, on the other hand, it's called hypoglycaemia, or a 'hypo'. Even if BGLs aren't so low that they classify as a hypo, at low levels they can make it unsafe to drive or operate other heavy machinery. A hypoglycaemic episode can usually be reversed by eating or drinking something sweet, or injecting a dose of the hormone glucagon, which rapidly raises BGL. If left untreated, however, a hypo can lead to shaking and trembling, headaches, dizziness, slurred speech, loss of consciousness, seizures and ultimately death.

'I've had lots of bad hypos,' Steph says. 'The first one was when I was ten. I fell unconscious – my parents weren't able to give me food because I was that out of it. They didn't want to give me the glucagon shot because they were scared they would do it wrong, so they called an ambulance. When it came, I couldn't even tell the paramedics my name. I was in hospital for a week or so after that.'

Another memorable hypo occurred while Steph was in her teens, when the drop in blood glucose levels befuddled her better judgement. 'In high school I once told a boy that I liked him, and we ended up dating. I don't know why I said that, because I really didn't like him at all!'

On another occasion, Steph was walking around the Sydney CBD on her own when her blood sugar began to plummet. She recalls feeling like she was intoxicated. 'I didn't know where I was going and I don't know how I ended up where I did. That's when it's scary – when you don't realise what you're doing or how you're doing it.'

Some people with type-1 diabetes have Impaired Awareness of Hypoglyceamia (IAH), which is also known as being hypo unaware. According to Diabetes Australia, IAH occurs when people don't feel the early warning symptoms of hypoglycaemia. It can be extremely dangerous, because by the time they realise they're in the grip of a hypo it can be hard to treat before they lose consciousness. The condition is more common among people who have had diabetes and hypos for many years.

Steph rarely experiences IAH unless she is distracted – as she was in 2015, when she was pregnant but didn't yet know it. (Hypoglycaemia is also more common during pregnancy.)

'During the first trimester your levels can go really low, because your body is working hard to create a baby. One day I had a hypo and my levels dropped to 0.8mmol/L, which is crazy low,' she says. 'Being that low is going-into-a-coma territory, but I was just talking normally.'

Whether a person is prone to hypo unawareness or not, Steph's experiences show that it's often safer to have somebody else around when BGLs start to drop, either to just provide snacks and drinks, or to call an ambulance if the episode develops into an emergency.

However, that somebody doesn't necessarily need to be a human. Since the early 2000s, many people with both type-1 and type-2 diabetes have been relying on trained diabetes-alert dogs to warn them of approaching hyper or hypoglycaemic episodes.

The first dog trained to detect hypoglycaemia, in 2003, was a Californian dog called Armstrong. Diabetes-alert dogs are trained to sniff out the chemical changes that occur in the human body as BGLs drop or increase, and they then alert the diabetic person (or their parent or guardian) so they can check their levels and take the necessary action.

Numerous charities now exist to provide alert dogs to both children and adults with diabetes, and training programs are available to people who want to train their own dogs to alert. In 2009, a six-year-old rescued border collie called Tinker became the United Kingdom's first official owner-trained diabetes alert dog. He was able to give his owner, Paul Jackson, up to thirty minutes warning of an impending hypo, and once dragged Paul home after he collapsed in the street.

Even more incredible than trained diabetes alert dogs are those that learn to alert without training. Canberra mum Adrienne Cottell's twin daughters, Hannah and Olivia Weber, were diagnosed with type-1 diabetes at two and six years of age. Adrienne used a video training program to teach the family dog, Molly Polly the Australian silky terrier, to alert to the girls' hypos – but Molly Polly taught herself to alert for *hyper*glycaemia and ketoacidosis.*

It never crossed Steph's mind to attempt to train Darcy and Chelsea to alert to her fluctuating BGLs – not

---

* You can read all about Molly Polly the diabetes-alert dog in my book *Dogs with Jobs*.

because she doubted her clever dogs could do it, but because she could already tell when a hypo was developing. 'Most of the time I do know a hypo is coming. I get really sweaty and feel really tired and can't do much. Then I start talking and talking and don't know what I'm saying.'

But as anyone who's ever had their dog follow them to the toilet will know, dogs don't always understand when their presence is not required. And if they do understand, they often don't care.

One evening in October 2011, Steph was preparing for dinner when she and her then husband began arguing. She had already administered the insulin needed to cover the carbohydrates she was about to consume for her evening meal, but she hadn't yet sat down to eat.

The early signs of a hypo began to appear. The trouble was that some of those signs – hunger, shaking, lightheadedness and mood swings – can also occur when we've missed a meal, while others crop up when we're embroiled in conflict. It was a double whammy for Steph; understandably, she didn't realise that her BGLs were dropping.

The couple's disagreement soon escalated into a heated quarrel, and Steph's husband left the house. Dinner was forgotten and the hypo started to really take hold.

'We were fighting and he decided to go out. He would have been able to warn me I was having a hypo, but his friends arrived and he went out with them. I was so upset that I went to bed without eating dinner.'

Being hungry meant that Steph's BGLs were already falling. The fact that she'd had insulin but not consumed the carbohydrates it was supposed to convert into energy meant her levels were pushed to a dangerous low.

In bed, famished and distressed, Steph quickly fell asleep. She was alone and teetering on the precipice of a life-threatening emergency. If she didn't wake up and eat or administer a glucagon injection soon, she would slip into a diabetic coma.

While she and her husband squabbled, Steph hadn't noticed where Darcy and Chelsea were. Nor did she see them as she retreated to the bedroom and dived beneath the covers. She doesn't know what her loyal companions were doing as she sank deeper into hypoglycaemia in her sleep. But when she was roused from slumber some time later, Chelsea was exactly where she needed to be: standing on Steph's chest.

'I either fell asleep or passed out. It must have been hours later that I woke up. Chelsea was standing over me with her tiny front paws on my chest, frantically licking my face and whining. It took me a while to realise what was going on. She was just trying her hardest to wake me up,' she says.

Chelsea, the fluffy terrier mix who weighed barely 5 kilograms, had brought Steph back from the brink, dragging her out of her hypoglycaemic blackout in the nick of time.

She had saved her human's life.

Who knows how much longer Steph could have slept before passing the point of no return? It's a question Chelsea was clearly not willing to learn the answer to.

To this day, Steph doesn't know what spurred her devoted dog into action that night. Chelsea was not a trained diabetes-alert dog and had never shown any inkling of being attuned to her owner's BGLs before. Did she detect the scent of plunging BGLs on Steph's breath? Did she hear that her breathing was becoming laboured or erratic? How could she have known that any of those scenarios meant danger?

How did Chelsea know it was up to her – and her alone – to do something before it was too late?

Even after Chelsea's frantic efforts brought her back to consciousness, Steph's BGLs were still critically low. She felt awful. It didn't register in that moment that Chelsea had likely plucked her from the jaws of death. All she could think about was regaining her equilibrium.

'Because it was a particularly bad hypo, I was just thinking, *I need something to eat.* I was so low and so out of it. I was drenched in sweat, dazed and barely able to move. Thankfully there was a packet of lollies on the bedside table next to me. I grabbed a handful and scoffed them down until I began to feel normal again,' she says. 'Any person with type-1 diabetes who has experienced a hypo like this knows how terrifying it can be. Unfortunately, many don't wake up like I did. It didn't occur to me at the time that Chelsea had saved my life. It didn't sink in until later.'

When the reality of what Chelsea had done for her did hit home, Steph was overwhelmed – not only by the terrifying thought of how close she had come to the unthinkable, but by the courage and tenacity her little dog had shown. She never would have expected it, but Chelsea did it anyway.

Steph had saved Chelsea's life by adopting her from the pound, and now her four-legged friend had returned the favour.

'It just made me feel so thankful. I always knew she was a great little dog, but after that I thought she was even greater,' she says. 'It's a cliché, but dogs really are man's best friend. They're just lovely. They show such empathy – well, Chelsea does anyway – and they just love life.'

Even more incredible than her life-saving feat is the fact that Chelsea has never again appeared to acknowledge Steph's BGLs in the decade since that frightening night. Steph has had hypos in Chelsea's presence since then – though thankfully none that were as severe – but if the brave terrier is aware of them, she doesn't let on.

It's as if she was granted a superpower for one night only and has no further need for it.

'I now have a continuous glucose monitor, which cuts off my insulin pump if my levels are going too low, and that makes it easier. But sometimes hypos are unavoidable. It's just something I've had to learn to live with,' Steph says.

Later, Steph divorced her husband and moved back in with her parents. Darcy and Chelsea came too, of course. She fell in love again, marrying Geoff in 2015, and welcomed daughters Mariella and Hannah.

When Steph and Geoff set up a home together, the property they rented did not allow pets. Fortunately, her parents were happy to take care of their 'granddogs' until the couple moved to a pet-friendly home.

They eventually found one, but it wasn't in Steph's native Sydney. In March 2019 they moved to Brisbane, where they could afford a house with a backyard for Darcy and Chelsea.

There was just one problem.

'My mum didn't want to give them up,' Steph says with a laugh. 'We were sending them money every month for food and things for the dogs, but they told us to stop and said they were happy to look after them. It was hard, but knowing they were so well looked after made it easier to move without them.'

Chelsea is now twelve, and she's living her best life in Sydney. Steph and her family visit often. Sadly, Darcy's adventure-filled life came to an end in October 2021. He was an impressive fourteen years old.

'Chelsea has put on weight since staying at my parents' house because they feed her so much! Mum walks her every day, so she loves it there.'

Chelsea deserves to spend her golden years being indulged and adored. She's earned it, not only because she saved Steph's life, but because she has loved Steph for the entire time she's known her.

A dog's capacity for love is limitless, and we should be amazed by that every single day.

Billy

The quiet hero

There are dog people, and then there are Dog People.

Lower-case dog people love dogs. They probably have a dog or two. They enjoy taking their canine companions for walks and snuggling on the sofa with them at night. Any dog would be lucky to spend his or her life with a lower-case dog person.

Dog People, however, are a different type entirely. They *really* love dogs. They have at least two, and often many more, all of which sleep on the humans' bed at night, despite having their pick of couches and plush dog beds all over the house. They volunteer with rescue groups and animal welfare charities. Their clothes are always covered in fur, and they always have poop bags and treats in their pockets. Their birthday and Christmas gifts are dog-themed every single year.

Dog People can never say no to a pooch in need, so

they foster or adopt the 'special cases' that others turn away. Their hearts shatter every time a dog in their care passes away, whether they've loved that dog for a week or a decade. And yet they sign up to do it again and again and again.

Lisa Weber is very much a Dog Person.

Her love of dogs was ignited early in life by her family's much-loved corgi, Minnie. She was by Lisa's side throughout her childhood and really 'formed my love for dogs,' she says. She was about fifteen when Minnie passed away.

While Minnie had been purchased from a breeder, Lisa's mum, Linda, decided that the family's next pet should be a rescue dog. She took Lisa and her sister to the RSPCA shelter at Lonsdale, south of Adelaide.

'We adopted Chester, a Maltese cross. He was our first rescue dog,' she says of the pup, who was just six months old when they rescued him. 'Later in life he had everything wrong with him. He became deaf and lost both of his eyes to disease. Chester was a beloved pet, so we tried everything we could, and he lived a long time. He was about fifteen when he died, so he had a good innings.'

Lisa had well and truly moved out of home by the time Chester passed away, and lived in a succession of share-houses that she felt weren't really appropriate for dogs. She had been grateful she could pop back to the family home to see Chester whenever she needed dog cuddles, but she deeply missed having a constant canine companion.

When she moved into her own rented apartment in Adelaide's inner north in her mid-twenties, Lisa knew it was time for a dog of her own. She wasn't looking that hard, nor did she have any particular criteria for her perfect pet – she was quite content to wait until she crossed paths with the right dog. She knew she would recognise the right one when she met them. Dog People always do.

Lisa didn't have to wait long. In 2013, a friend who worked at a veterinary hospital got in touch. A 10-year-old Lhasa Apso had been brought in needing major dental work, but her owners were unable to afford it. They had asked the clinic to euthanise the sweet dog instead, believing it was their only option.

'The owners thought she only needed a minor dental treatment, but it turned out all her teeth needed to be removed,' says Lisa.

It later emerged that rotten teeth were only part of 'Princess's' problems – though she was a senior dog, she was not toilet trained. Lisa suspected she had never spent much time outside.

Rather than put her to sleep – Princess was healthy apart from the appalling state of her teeth – the vet told the owners he could take the dog and find her a new, loving home. They agreed.

'That's how I got the call. And that's what started my senior dog journey,' Lisa says.

She decided to give the pretty little girl a new name to mark the start of her new life, and so Princess became

Peaches. She and Lisa instantly became inseparable, as Lisa worked hard to introduce her to all the things she had missed out on.

'Through Peaches I learned what it was truly like to rescue a dog. We'd had Chester, but it was different with Peaches. Being a naive 25-year-old, I didn't actually think people could treat dogs the way she had been treated,' she says. 'I had to teach her to go to the toilet outside, teach her how to walk on a lead. She would come with me everywhere. She had no teeth, but she had so much sass.'

Peaches even inspired Lisa to make a career change. Previously working in finance, she spied a job vacancy at the RSPCA soon after adopting her scrappy little sidekick and decided to go for it.

'Honestly, Peaches inspired me to go for that job. I never thought I'd work for a rescue, let alone the RSPCA, but I was there for eight-and-a-half years.' She started as the office manager and held a variety of roles, working as a business partner in human resources by the time she left the charity for a new career in mid-2022.

Not surprisingly, the RSPCA's Adelaide HQ is a dog-friendly workplace, so Peaches was able to go to work with Lisa most days. (Office staff at the Lonsdale shelter often also bring anxious dogs from the kennels into the office during the day to give them a break.)

'All the staff members' dogs got along, and it was really cool. Peaches was awesome – everybody loved her.

She had a bed in my office and a bed at home,' says Lisa.

It was once she started working at the RSPCA that Lisa found her true calling as a Dog Person: she became the go-to foster carer for the small senior dogs that needed a little extra TLC, or that didn't cope well in the shelter environment.

A year after joining the charity, in March 2015, she adopted a second dog. Macca was a teenage Lhasa Apso–Maltese mix whose owners had passed away. As members of the RSPCA's Care for Life program, his owners had left the organisation a bequest in their wills in exchange for lifetime care for Macca after they died.

Once again, it was Peaches who convinced Lisa to act. 'Peaches was probably about thirteen, and I wasn't necessarily looking for another dog, but as soon as Macca met Peaches they fell in love,' she recalls. 'I was like, "Oh, do you want a friend?" They were inseparable. It was the best marriage of dogs I've ever seen.'

Their devotion to each other was a little surprising, since they were like chalk and cheese in temperament. Peaches was all attitude, while Macca was a more sombre character. 'He walked with a bit of a waddle and always had a sad expression on his face, like the *Winnie the Pooh* character Eeyore.'

But Macca was anything but sad. He and Peaches spent a blissful eleven months together, until she passed away in February 2016 at the age of fourteen.

'Peaches would have seizures, which developed about a year after I adopted her. The vets couldn't work out why,' says Lisa. 'On this particular day, I was in the shower and she was having a really big seizure. Macca was trying to get my attention: he was scratching at the bathroom door, trying to tell me something was wrong. I wish I'd got out of the shower straight away, but I didn't.'

The moment she discovered Peaches in the grip of the prolonged seizure, Lisa rushed her to the emergency vet hospital. Staff there were able to control the seizure with medication, but every time they attempted to reduce the dose the seizures would begin again.

Ultimately, Lisa had to make the heartbreaking decision to let her sweet girl go. Her death was devastating for both Lisa and Macca.

'Macca was heartbroken without Peaches. I have this photo of him looking lost, looking around the backyard trying to find her,' she says. 'Because Peaches was the first dog who was all mine, she was the hardest to say goodbye to.'

Although she worked at the RSPCA, Lisa's job never involved direct contact with animals. After losing Peaches, she also started volunteering at the Lonsdale shelter as a dog walker. 'Macca was nearing fifteen and he had never been a let's-get-up-and-go-walking kind of dog. I knew the shelter was struggling for volunteers so I thought, *It's just a little extra something I can do, and it's enjoyable.*'

It was during one of these volunteer shifts that Lisa met another pint-sized pooch in desperate need of patience and understanding.

Peggy-Sue was a two-year-old Chihuahua. She had been found abandoned in a rental property after her owners moved out. She displayed anti-social behaviour in the RSPCA shelter, and staff were not at all confident she would do well in a behaviour assessment, which all RSPCA rescue dogs must pass in order to be deemed suitable for adoption.

'She's not well socialised with other dogs. She can't be on a lead. She'll probably give you a nip if you try to pick her up,' Lisa explains.

But the more time she spent with Peggy-Sue, the more Lisa felt the little dog could thrive with the right owner. 'Every Saturday I would sit in her kennel and she'd just sit on my lap and I'd pat her. Peggy-Sue was a gentle dog.'

Plus, she couldn't help but feel that Peaches might have had a hand – or paw – in bringing her and Peggy-Sue together.

'One thing that really drew me to Peggy-Sue was that the day the RSPCA had assigned as her birthday was the same day that Peaches passed away. That was kind of a sign. I thought, *I'm going to adopt Peggy-Sue. I'm going to try to help her.*'

And so Peggy-Sue went home with Lisa and Macca. In truth, Lisa was a little concerned about whether Macca would bond with his new housemate. Not just because

Peggy-Sue had already shown she wasn't fond of most other dogs, but also because Macca was still desperately missing Peaches.

But her worries were unfounded. After some initial trepidation, Macca and Peggy-Sue became best friends. And surprisingly, it was Peggy-Sue that led the way.

'At the start Macca was like, *Who is this dog?* But soon he had a best friend again. It turns out Peggy-Sue gets fully attached to other little dogs,' says Lisa. 'I don't know if maybe she was only temperament tested with big dogs, but she really, *really* bonds with small dogs. She snuggles into them.'

With Macca and Peggy-Sue established as the resident A-team, Lisa signed up to foster other small dogs in need. Indi, Lucy, Betty and Maggie all got to swap the RSPCA shelter for comfy beds in the family home for various lengths of time before finding their forever homes. While Macca was tolerant of his foster siblings, he was not especially interested in them. Peggy-Sue, on the other hand, became a doting den mother of sorts.

'Peggy-Sue was good with the fosters because she would calm their anxiety. They had always come from bad homes or been mistreated, and it was like she would reassure them and say, *This person is okay, this home is okay,*' Lisa says. 'She would vouch for us.'

Peggy-Sue was particularly attached to Indi, who stayed for nearly four months, and was bereft when she moved on to her forever family.

'She got really sad when we had to say goodbye to Indi. I was saying, "It's okay, you've still got Macca,"' she says. 'If I'd known what was going to happen in the future, I would have adopted Indi.'

What happened was that fate dealt another tough blow. In September 2017, Macca died. Just as he had mourned when Peaches passed away, Peggy-Sue grieved deeply for her best mate.

Lisa started taking Peggy-Sue to work each day because she felt the loving Chihuahua was too glum to be left at home on her own. 'Peggy-Sue was extra needy after Macca died. She would cry during the day – our neighbours heard her – and she had never really been a crying dog before that. She was a little pocket rocket, so when she was mopey, I knew she was down.'

It was clear to Lisa what she had to do. 'I knew I needed to get another dog for Peggy-Sue, there was no doubt about that, but my heart was like, *I don't know if I can do it again.*'

She thought she might be able to protect her battered heart if she steered clear of seniors and only committed to fostering, not adoption.

'I was saying to everyone at work, "I'm not having another senior! I'll foster, but I'm not adopting another senior!"' Lisa says with a chuckle.

None of her co-workers believed her for a moment.

*

Limited office space at the RSPCA Lonsdale shelter meant some corporate staff didn't have assigned offices or even desks; they simply set up for the day wherever there was room. One advantage of this desk-hopping was that there were always new dogs to meet, as different adoptable dogs from the shelter would hang out in the office during the day.

One day in November 2017, Lisa found herself sharing her workspace with an adorable 'little white fluffball dog' that was appropriately named Snowball. It had been almost three months since Macca passed away and Peggy-Sue was still pining for her pal. Lisa wondered whether Snowball might be a suitable new friend for her bereaved pup.

Lisa spoke to the shelter manager and learned that Snowball was an adult dog who was ready for adoption. So at the end of the workday, after Snowball had been returned to her shelter enclosure, Lisa decided to pay her a one-on-one visit.

'I thought I'd go down and say goodbye to her. On the way, I ran into a friend who's a kennel hand in the shelter, and I told her that I might adopt Snowball.' Lisa's friend had other ideas. 'She said, "Nope! You have to meet this other guy – he's just come in, and he'll be perfect for you. You're really good with dogs like him."'

Protecting her bruised heart, and adamant she wasn't going to adopt another elderly dog, Lisa broached the all-important question: was he a senior dog? Her friend said, 'Just come and meet him.'

She followed her friend to the shelter, where she was introduced to a dog called Billy.

At least, Lisa assumed Billy was a dog. He was in such appalling condition that it was virtually impossible to tell what he was at first glance.

RSPCA Inspector Craig Dawe had seized Billy from a dilapidated and rubbish-strewn house in Adelaide's northern suburbs just that morning. 'I vividly remember seeing him that first time, lying in his kennel with a look of total defeat on his face, his head resting on his two front paws,' Dawe told *SA Life* magazine in 2019. 'I called him and he raised his dirty, matted face and stared at me for a few seconds. It wasn't until I crouched down and called him over again that his tail began to wag and he walked over to me. It was like he initially couldn't believe someone was actually talking to him and paying him some attention . . . it really broke my heart.'

As Lisa understands it, Billy was owned by a woman who had lived at the house with her adult son. When his mother abruptly moved out, the man apparently refused to take care of the pet she had left behind.

Ten-year-old Billy was banished to the overgrown backyard. He lived without food, water or shelter for months before his neglect was reported to the RSPCA. He had been eating anything he could find and was severely malnourished.

Billy's fur was matted, filled with grass seeds and infested with fleas; he would have been in awful discomfort. He was apparently a Maltese terrier mix, but when Lisa first met him she couldn't even tell what colour he was. 'They had to shave him so close to his skin because he was so matted and had been riddled with fleas for so long. He was just skin and bone.'

He didn't even move as his fur was being shaved. He simply lay still, his spirit broken.

Beyond his terrible physical neglect, darling Billy was also utterly, utterly terrified. 'It was the day from hell for him. He was so scared, he was in a little cocoon. His little head was buried and he was just shaking. I couldn't even see his eyes,' says Lisa.

In an instant, her mind was made up: Billy would not spend a single night in the shelter. He was coming home with her.

'My heart broke. I thought, I'm taking him home. I knew that he had a long recovery ahead of him that would not be possible in the shelter – especially the mental recovery,' she says. 'He needed to do his recovery with me.'

At the time Lisa was building her dream home in the Adelaide Hills, so she and Peggy-Sue were living with Lisa's mum, Linda. (Funnily enough, Linda also had a dog called Billy.) Lisa had already let Linda know that Snowball would likely be coming home with her that evening, but she arrived with Billy instead. (Don't worry about Snowball – she was also quickly adopted by an adoring family.)

'Mum said, "This doesn't look like the dog you described." I hadn't committed to adopting Billy at that stage. I just wanted him to recover. My previous foster, Indi, had been in pretty poor condition as well when she came to me, so I thought, *I can just do that again with Billy.*'

But after everything he'd been through, Billy was understandably slow to trust his loving new home. Even the caring presence of Peggy-Sue didn't seem to help him settle in.

'He just wouldn't come out of his shell,' says Lisa. 'He was always a timid dog. He just liked his own space. I don't think he'd had many – or any – affectionate interactions with his previous owners.'

Soon after his arrival, Billy developed a cough. Lisa took him to the vet, who discovered seven fossilised grass seeds embedded deep in his ear canal that were irritating his ears, nasal passages and throat. He must have been in extreme pain for a very long time.

Once the seeds were extracted, Billy was transformed.

'It was such a relief for him. He came out of his shell immediately. He was jumping around the backyard – I'd never seen him that happy. I feel like he was a lot more confident after that. He was like a different dog,' she says. 'It was surreal to see his progress. Then his fur started growing back and it was like, "Oh! You're a white dog!"'

RSPCA Inspector Craig Dawe was also blown away by Billy's top-to-toe makeover.

'It was like he was reborn and his personality started to come back. He turned into a sprightly boy with a prance in his step,' he told *SA Life*. 'I was amazed, as I'd thought we were treating an old, decrepit dog on his last legs.'

Billy blossomed so much over the next few months that he even began to reciprocate Peggy-Sue's gentle affection. Not only that, by the time he moved into Lisa's new home, he had additional family members to fall in love with: Lisa had met her partner, Trasden Kowalick, in mid-2018, and the following year the couple welcomed their first child, son Harrison.

'Both Billy and Peggy-Sue used to sleep on the bed with us, but the first time Harrison woke up in the night, Peggy-Sue started barking,' she says. 'I thought, *This isn't going to work*. So from then on they slept on the sofa together.

'I think once that happened Billy realised, *Okay, Peggy-Sue is my little cuddler*. Peggy-Sue is such a helpful dog and she definitely made him feel at ease. I started bringing them both to work with me.'

Somewhere along the line, Billy's status in the family changed from 'only staying until he gets better' to 'here for life'. Despite Lisa's fears that she wouldn't cope with losing another senior pet, she fell head over heels in love with Billy anyway. 'I didn't want to make the mistake of not adopting him like I had with Indi,' she says.

And she wasn't the only one whose heart Billy had well and truly captured. His metamorphosis from scared, mistreated afterthought to happy and confident family pet was so remarkable that he became something of an RSPCA poster boy. His new lease on life was testament to the importance of rescue, and the power of patience and loving kindness.

In 2019, Billy was named RSPCA SA's Hero Dog and chosen to be the ambassador for that year's Million Paws Walk. The annual walk is the RSPCA's biggest fundraising event, raising millions of dollars for the charity since its inception in 1991. The money raised is vital in keeping RSPCA shelters open and RSPCA inspectors on the road all around Australia. Each state branch nominates a Hero Dog to attend a local walk as a living embodiment of the charity's commitment to animals.

Lisa says Billy was completely deserving of the SA accolade. 'I was very happy to share his story, because it was probably one of the worst examples of neglect and mistreatment that RSPCA SA had seen that year. It was just good to share the story of how far he'd come. The photos of when I first got him compared to how he had progressed – his fur growing back, getting along with Peggy-Sue – were really remarkable.'

Billy didn't actually complete the walk. He was reactive towards other dogs, and Lisa was worried he would become overwhelmed and it would jeopardise his recovery, so instead he enjoyed the festivities from the comfort of her arms.

As was Billy's quiet way, he didn't let his celebrity status go to his head. After his star turn as a Million Paws

Ambassador, he was more than happy to retreat from the limelight and resume his contented life with Lisa, Trasden, Harrison and Peggy-Sue.

In early 2021, when Billy was around fifteen years old, he was diagnosed with canine cognitive dysfunction, which affects dogs in a similar way to Alzheimer's disease in humans. The condition progressed with frightening speed; it was agonising for Lisa to witness her brave little dog's decline.

'The worst day was when he got stuck between the laundry trough and the washing machine and couldn't get out. He didn't know where he was,' she says. 'At night-time he would do laps around our kitchen island for hours. I'd get up and put him back to bed and he would get out and start doing it again.'

Though it was devastating for her to acknowledge, Lisa knew she simply couldn't continue to let Billy suffer. He had already been through so much and had demonstrated his resilience – and his trust in her – time and time again. He had more than earned a rest.

'It went on for a while before my partner said, "We need to do something about Billy." The vets gave him medication, but it wasn't helping. It was getting dangerous to leave him home alone,' she explains. 'It was bad and I knew his quality of life was suffering.'

From the day she agreed to meet him against her

better instincts, Lisa had made so many good decisions for Billy. On 30 May 2021, she made her last, best decision for him.

She hadn't been able to be with Peaches and Macca when they passed away because they had been medical emergencies, but she was determined to be by Billy's side, loving and comforting him until his final breath. She will be forever grateful for that opportunity.

'The vets let me hold him and it was such a beautiful experience. I got to say goodbye properly and he slowly drifted away in my arms,' she says. She was newly pregnant with her second son, Freddie, and is sad that he never got to meet brave little Billy.

All the amazing dogs Lisa has shared her life with have left paw prints on her heart. She has continued to foster since Billy passed away. But there was something extra special about the diminutive Maltese cross, discarded like trash only to become a confident and loving family member. It was as though destiny brought them together.

'I loved going to the kennels at the shelter, but it also broke my heart, so I'd been avoiding it a bit after losing Macca. The day I met Billy, I wouldn't have even gone down there if it wasn't for Snowball being in the office,' says Lisa. 'Something happened that made us meet, for sure. He was such a sweet dog. He had the most beautiful eyes and they would just stare into my soul. Sometimes I thought, *Is he looking at me to say thank you?*'

He probably was. *Thank you for rescuing me. Thank you for taking that chance even when your heart was still aching for Macca. Thank you for giving me time and patience and kindness. Thank you for allowing me to become the dog I was always meant to be.*

Thank you for being amazing, and thank you for showing me that I was amazing, too.

Grover

The literary muse

Human beings have an enormous capacity for delusion. We can convince ourselves of all sorts of wonderful things, even in the face of often overwhelming evidence to the contrary.

Studies have shown that most people believe in at least one conspiracy theory, with aliens, ghosts and other paranormal phenomena at the top of the list. Around 40 per cent of us think we are uniquely gifted geniuses surrounded by foolish people who don't recognise our talents. And an embarrassingly large percentage of the population believes that a celebrity is secretly in love with us. Cringe.

But perhaps the wildest delusion we've all bought into is that we choose our pets. We think that we go to a shelter, breeder or pet shop armed with a list of criteria and select the animal that ticks most of the boxes. We tell ourselves we're in control.

News flash: we're not.

We don't choose our animal companions. They choose us.

Every. Single. Time.

We always get the pets we need at the precise moments we need them. Sometimes it might even look like they need us, but we always need them more. They may rely on us for a full belly, a warm place to sleep and veterinary care, but *we* are dependent on them for the lessons that loving and protecting them provide.

Claire Garth has always known this. She has been chosen by some remarkable animals in her life, although at times she almost believed she was doing the choosing.

'I grew up in Melbourne with a menagerie of animals. I had long-suffering parents who were great to me and my three siblings – we wanted all the pets in the world,' says Claire with a laugh.

The first pet to choose Claire's family was Minnie, an adorable black-and-white 'bitser' dog who simply turned up one day and never left.

'She was a rescue of sorts in that she was found. Back in the day I'm not sure there were policies for taking lost dogs to the vet and getting them scanned for a microchip. I'm not even sure if there were microchips. If you found a lost dog, you kept it,' she says. 'No one came to claim her, so she became our dog.'

Loving Minnie was a formative experience. 'I don't remember not having her and I don't remember her coming to us. She was just part of the family before I was. The idea that you can fall in love with any dog started early for me.'

She was devastated when the sweet dog passed away from old age. Her younger siblings had come along by then and it wasn't long before they were pestering their parents for another four-legged family member. They duly took their kids to the Lost Dogs' Home to choose a new family dog – but once again, their new dog chose them.

'There were a bunch of dogs there and they all came up to the gate, desperately wanting to go home with us. But there was one dog that didn't get off his bed, a little Jack Russell terrier,' says Claire. 'My brother was about three and he was adamant that this was the dog that was coming home with us.'

The dog had indeed made his intentions clear: Claire's family would be *his* new family.

'My brother was allowed to name him, and he called him Buddy Boy.'

After Buddy Boy came Claire's terrier mix, Lulu. Well, technically she was Claire's dog – once she started working, she would carry Lulu on the train in her handbag and sneak her into her office every day – but Lulu ultimately chose different owners for herself.

'She was the dog my parents didn't want, but my dad became obsessed with her. Lulu didn't know she was a dog,' Claire says. 'When I moved out of home, she stayed behind. I moved in with a friend and couldn't really have a dog with me, and I didn't want to take Lulu away from Mum and Dad.'

Lulu died in mid-2022 at the grand old age of fifteen, having lived 'a fabulous life' with Claire's parents, including later becoming the favourite playmate of their eight grandchildren.

It would be five years after meeting Lulu before Claire was chosen by another dog. In the meantime, she qualified as a primary school teacher and met her partner, Andrew. Around 2007, she swapped teaching for the corporate sector, working for the government on major infrastructure projects. When Andrew was offered a new role in Sydney in 2012, the young couple jumped at the chance for a new adventure.

Claire was able to transfer her existing job to her new city, so she didn't need to worry about finding work. But that also meant she missed out on the chance to make friends with new colleagues. Andrew also travelled a lot for his job; sometimes Claire was able to accompany him, but sometimes she wasn't. It wasn't long before she felt that lack of a social network. Loneliness started to creep in.

'I knew no one in Sydney, and I felt like I needed to make some friends. I started looking for experiences where I would get to meet people. I can't remember how it popped up as an option, but something came up about volunteering at Sydney Dogs and Cats Home,' she says.

SDCH has been taking care of Sydney's lost, abandoned and neglected pets since 1946. It is Sydney's only charity pound and not-for-profit community animal facility, and takes in thousands of pets every year from multiple council areas across Sydney.

It seemed like the perfect fit for Claire. She and Andrew didn't have any pets of their own – it would have been unfair given their frequent travels – but she missed the company of animals. She signed up as a volunteer dog walker.

'That way I didn't have to have a dog but could still feel connected to animals, and I would be giving back to the community,' she explains. 'I would also meet people and make friends, and see a different part of Sydney.'

But the very first time she stepped foot inside SDCH, which was then located in the southern Sydney suburb of Carlton, Claire knew she had made a mistake. There was zero chance her involvement with the shelter would be just a casual arrangement.

'I knew the second I walked in there that it was going to be a lifelong relationship. I very quickly discovered what a unique place it was. Places like that just get you, and the people are so passionate,' she says. 'I fell in love with the organisation, and with almost every animal that walked through the door.'

She especially loved the fact that, unlike some pounds, SDCH is a no-kill shelter, meaning animals are never euthanised due to space restrictions or time limits. Instead, the facility cares for pets until they can either be reunited with their owners or placed in a suitable new home.

'In the rescue world there can be a lot of "this dog needs a home or it will die", and I feel like that can lead to dogs winding up in the wrong homes. They often end up back in the system, but with a bad rap,' says Claire. 'I really loved that they matched dogs, and cats as well, based on where they would thrive. They were really keen to make sure that when a dog got a home it was its forever home.'

Claire also made her first real Sydney friend at SDCH, forming 'an instant bond' with Amanda Stokes, the shelter's fundraising guru.

It wasn't long before Claire found herself wanting to do more for SDCH than just walking dogs. Her rented home wasn't suitable for dogs, but she thought kittens would be more manageable, so she became a foster carer. She would often have up to eight kittens at a time, all requiring round-the-clock care.

Then she and Andrew bought a house and from then, says Claire, 'it was game on'.

'We still had very busy lives and I was like, "Do I have time for a dog at the moment?" So we started by fostering a couple of little puppies. They weren't going to be the dogs for me, but I could still love them and get them back on their feet so they could go to their perfect homes,' she says. 'We sometimes had foster kittens and foster puppies at the same time – that was fun for my long-suffering partner!'

In 2013, Claire's dog-loving dreams came true when she was offered a paid position at SDCH. She had noticed while volunteering that the shelter had no social media presence, which had by then become a critical tool in building brand awareness for businesses and charities alike.

It was even more crucial for SDCH, which had just been served an eviction notice. The owner of their Carlton site intended to redevelop it; the shelter would have to go within months. Moving anywhere at all would be wildly expensive, and that was without even factoring in the cost of building the facilities needed to house up to 3000 animals per year.

'I started doing Instagram and Facebook for them to raise funds, but also to raise awareness. They needed a profile so people knew who they were. I knew that people who loved dogs would tag their friends in social media posts to say, "Hey, this looks like the dog for you,"' she says. 'It worked. Our engagement lifted, and I found myself with a job as public relations and marketing manager.'

Her new job also involved assisting with fundraising while her friend Amanda was on maternity leave. When Amanda returned to work, Claire became SDCH's general manager.

Space at the shelter was limited, which meant staff meetings were usually held wherever there was room. One frigid winter's day in 2014, the team was crowded into the consulting room of the shelter's vet when an animal control officer from a council arrived with a dog.

This was an everyday – sometimes multiple times a day – occurrence at SDCH. 'There was a constant flow of dogs being brought in and the rangers all knew the process,' says Claire.

Dogs that were simply lost, because they had escaped their backyard or slipped their lead at the dog park, were rarely injured. They would be sent to a kennel to think about their cheeky behaviour for a while before being quickly reclaimed by their frantic owners.

The council rangers knew, however, to bring any animal that was injured or appeared unwell straight to the vet.

That was the case that June morning. The ranger walked into the vet's room with an emaciated border collie in his arms.

'He said, "He was running down the street and he's not okay."' As the vet went about getting ready to examine him, the ranger put the dog on the examination table, and he just collapsed,' Claire recalls. 'We all lurched forward. I slipped his little head under my arm. He just sort of looked at me and I thought, *Oh gosh, I'm in a lot of trouble – he's going to be mine.*'

Claire had been chosen, and she knew it.

The exhausted dog was in terrible shape. Though he was an adult, he weighed just 9 kilograms; a fully grown male border collie should weigh up to 20 kilograms.

He also had a thick, broken chain around his neck. It wasn't a dog collar – Claire had only ever seen chains of that size wrapped around gates and secured with hefty padlocks.

'He was completely covered in fleas – they were jumping off him. He was missing massive chunks of fur, and he was so skinny you could see his bones,' she says.

As is the protocol, the dog was scanned for a microchip. Claire was sure he would not have one. He had to be a stray. No pet owner responsible enough to chip their dog could possibly allow him to be in such atrocious condition. Right?

Wrong. The dog did have a microchip. Even more surprisingly, the contact details were up to date. Most shocking of all, he was not a stray. He was five years old and had escaped from his home – and the owner wanted him back.

Claire went straight into protective mode. 'I said, "There is no way this dog is going back to where he came from," I was already planning to put him into witness protection.'

The vet agreed. The RSPCA was notified and they confiscated the dog from the owner, pending investigation. The dog would remain in the care of SDCH until the matter was resolved, which would likely take months.

There was no way the dog could survive a cold winter in the shelter in his condition. He was simply too weak.

'The vet clocked that I was the biggest softie in the place and said, "You've got this brand-new house just around the corner – can he stay with you until he's a little stronger?" We'd only been in the house two weeks – we hadn't even unpacked – but I said, "Sure."'

She snapped a quick picture of her new foster dog on her phone and sent it to Andrew, writing, *This little guy needs a place to stay for a couple of days.*

Andrew's response was swift and unequivocal: *BRING HIM HOME.*

She did exactly that.

Her first task was to give him a new name, one that represented the beginning of his new life. When she had been fostering kittens, Claire had named them after American Presidents – a nod to Andrew's card-carrying status as a 'US politics tragic'. She decided to continue the tradition with her new foster friend.

'We'd had a Woodrow and a Lincoln, et cetera. We talked through a few options and settled on Grover,' she says. 'I was really focused on having him gain weight and I believe President Grover Cleveland was quite plump, so I saw it as aspirational.'

Claire's new pup had never responded to his previous name, but he picked up 'Grover' within a day.

As the RSPCA pursued Grover's owner through the courts, Claire was able to glean some information about what the brave pooch had endured. She learned that RSPCA inspectors had found another dog at the owner's property and that it had displayed aggressive behaviour.

Claire surmised that Grover was intended to be a guard dog, but what she had seen of his sweet and loving nature so far suggested 'he would not have made a good guard dog in any shape or form'. It appeared that the second dog was bought as a replacement and Grover was relegated to the backyard, where he was chained to a clothesline.

'We think he'd been chained up for most of his life. He'd barked himself hoarse in that backyard, where he'd been out in all the elements. He also had a really bad skin condition,' she says. 'I assume they fed him occasionally, because he was alive, but certainly not often and not enough.'

She couldn't understand why the owner was fighting the RSCPA in court when it was abundantly clear he did not care for Grover.

'I think he just didn't want to have a record of being a neglectful dog owner. He fought but the RSPCA won, and I believe he was convicted of animal neglect and told he could never own an animal again,' she says. 'It was probably good that I was at arm's length from all that. My job was just to take care of him.'

Grover technically remained a foster dog for the duration of the court case, but Claire knew from the moment she laid eyes on him that he was hers for keeps.

'I knew immediately that he was staying. After the first couple of days I said, "He just needs a week more." Then it became, "A couple of days more." But Andrew and

I both knew. There was just no doubt in our minds that he was our dog. We started loving him from day one.'

His official 'gotcha day' was the day Claire received word that the RSPCA had won its case and she could adopt Grover. But really, she knew that day had come months earlier, when Grover looked into her eyes as he lay on the examination table and picked her.

What she didn't know, however, was that the best was yet to come.

As thrilled as Claire was that Grover was now hers for good, her extensive experience with rescue animals told her that a dog didn't survive five years of unimaginable cruelty and neglect without gaining a few scars.

Grover's physical condition improved dramatically in a short space of time thanks to their attentive care, but his emotional trauma would be a tougher nut to crack. He had a collection of phobias that would be triggered when she least expected it.

'He was petrified of anyone wearing work boots. And water – I remember the first time I got the hose out to water the garden and he just lost it. He would walk around puddles, and we had to buy him a raincoat,' says Claire.

Grover rarely barked after his adoption because he had severely damaged vocal cords. She suspects he barked incessantly in his old life to gain attention or relief from his ravenous hunger, and would be drenched with the hose in an effort to silence him.

He also had severe separation anxiety – as Claire discovered when she first started to leave him at home alone for short periods.

'We set up a camera to watch him, and he would just pace from room to room and scratch at the front door. That's how he ended up with a job at the shelter,' she says. 'He would come into work with me each day and just sleep in a bed at my feet.'

Grover wasn't the first dog to find respite in the SDCH office. Senior dogs, and those that were unwell or stressed by the kennel environment, would often spend part of their day there – but Grover was the first dog to turn it into a bona fide job.

'We found that having Grover in there would calm the other dogs that came in. They would curl up in the bed together. He was really good at calming down puppies that were crazy or senior dogs that were frightened,' says Claire. 'It went from, *This is how we can help him with his separation anxiety*, to, *We need him because he's performing a real job here.*'

On one occasion, Grover appointed himself guide dog to a blind Pomeranian called Benji, leading him to the office bed so they could nap together.

'I feel like border collies want a job. That's true of all working dogs, I think. I don't think he would have been able to go out there and herd sheep, but he absolutely loved doing stuff. He just had this streak through him that was very caring, particularly with other animals. He was quite miraculous.'

Partly because of his separation anxiety, but mostly just because they loved his company, Claire and Andrew took Grover almost everywhere with them, including to their favourite local cafés. In the early days, however, he looked so unwell that he would draw shocked looks from passers-by.

Claire found herself regaling strangers with Grover's incredible tale of transformation just so they wouldn't think she was responsible for his appalling condition.

'Next thing you know, people would be ordering plates of bacon for him. I've had chefs come out with a burger for Grover and I've said I didn't order it and they've said, "That lady over there did,"' she says. 'I'd look over and people would just be sobbing.'

The more she told Grover's story, the more she realised his remarkable recovery truly moved people.

'It was a story that seemed to resonate with people. One day it struck me that there was a book idea here. His was a story that needed to be told.'

Claire had never seriously considered writing a book before, but in her former career as a primary school teacher she had seen that books and reading could have a profound effect on children.

'I taught a lot of kids at varying levels who needed a lot of extra attention and love,' she says. 'I loved reading to kids more than anything and found that it was probably the most powerful tool to convey anything to a child.'

Claire decided to write a picture book about Grover's metamorphosis from mistreated and malnourished to beloved family pet. She arranged a meeting with an independent Australian publisher to pitch her idea – and, of course, she took Grover with her.

'I had all my notes about how this book would help kids and all the key themes: making friends, starting over. The publisher spent the whole time patting Grover – I'm not sure she listened to any of it!'

But she did listen, because an hour later she rang Claire with a proposal.

'She said, "We love it but we think it should be for older readers, we think it should be a chapter book, and we want you to write three,"' Claire recalls. 'I was like, "What?!" But it made sense. The themes I could cover in a chapter book were really quite deep, especially resilience.'

Soon after their initial offer, the publisher signed up two more books. The Grover McBane: Rescue Dog series would now have five books in total.

Claire knuckled down and started to write the first book, *Grover Finds a Home*, but almost immediately she found herself struggling for a reason she didn't expect.

'I took me forever to write the first book because I found it so emotional. To do it well, I had to relive it, and probably in a way that I didn't do when it was actually happening. I had to really get into Grover's mindset,' she admits. 'I knew I had to persist, because it gave me a really good understanding of where he'd come from and how miraculous it was that he'd come out the other side. I also needed to fully understand it myself so that I could write it in a way that was palatable for seven- to ten-year-old readers, so that they wouldn't get two pages in and be too scared to continue.'

The positive side of coming to terms with the magnitude of what Grover had overcome was that it made writing the next four books 'so much fun' for Claire. It also deepened the bond she shared with him.

'Our connection definitely grew. Our bond strengthened. I honestly feel like I got a real feel for how he would talk and how he would think,' Claire says. 'I joke that Grover wrote the books and I just helped him with the typing.'

When the first book hit shelves in 2016, the response was immediate. Children loved reading about Grover's adventures with his friends – one book even includes his pal Benji the Pomeranian – and they really connected with the themes of feeling like a fish out of water and overcoming adversity.

Claire and Grover were in hot demand, and together they visited schools up and down Australia's east coast. One of the moments that really touched Claire's heart was meeting a young student who was a Syrian refugee. Grover, who always had a special affinity for children, seemed to understand that the little boy needed his love.

'I'd given a talk about resilience and how Grover had to start over and make new friends. I'd spoken about Grover going up to all these dogs in the dog park and trying to make friends, and how hard that is when everybody's already got their friends,' she says. 'This little boy threw his arms around Grover and gave him a hug. Then he turned to the teacher and said, "He's just like me." He was starting over too.'

Grover received fan letters from kids all over the world. He also collected several thousand followers on the Instagram account Claire set up for him.

She knew from the moment she laid eyes on Grover that he was a very special dog, but it was surreal that so many strangers thought so too. 'There were many occasions where I'd realise that other people thought my dog was the best dog. I did have moments where I'd think, *This is MY dog having this really profound effect on all these people.*'

Grover was ten years old when his books were published. Claire, Andrew and their daughter, Ivy, hoped for many more years with him. After all he'd been through in the first half of his life, he deserved a long and happy second act.

Tragically, it wasn't to be.

In 2019, Grover started to become a little unsteady on his feet. He was slower than usual and didn't seem to want to run around as much. He'd had arthritis almost as long as he had lived with Claire, and he also had brittle bones due to the malnutrition he'd experienced in his early life. These conditions had been well managed with supplements and therapeutic massage, yet Grover seemed to be getting worse.

There was something else going on.

Grover's regular vet referred him to Sydney's Small Animal Specialist Hospital for tests. Claire was stunned by the eventual diagnosis: Grover had an inoperable tumour on his spine.

She and Andrew discussed treatment options with Grover's team of specialists, but there was no cure for his cancer. They opted instead for medication that would buy him some time and keep him comfortable. Meanwhile they tried to prepare themselves for the inevitable goodbye.

Claire couldn't help but feel ripped off on Grover's behalf. He'd had so many adventures and made up for lost time in myriad wonderful ways, but there was still so much she wanted him to experience. The thought that he wouldn't get that opportunity was unbearable.

So she got creative. Claire drew up a bucket list for Grover that included as many fun activities as she could think of.

'I thought of all these things that he might like to do, like eat a whole cheese pizza, stay in a swanky hotel, and be in a room surrounded by tennis balls,' she says. 'I think it was a coping mechanism for me, more than anything else.'

She also threw him a farewell party and invited family, friends, and his entire Instagram following. Several hundred people came to honour Grover and thank him for all the joy he had brought to their lives, whether through his books, his Instagram pictures or simply his existence.

'I remember thinking that I was probably the kind of person who would go to a random dog's party, but for that to be *my* dog was crazy.'

Claire and Andrew had made a promise that they would only continue Grover's treatment for as long as it maintained his quality of life. He still loved food and people, and he still wanted to catch his favourite tennis ball, and they would do everything they could for him for as long as that was the case.

But one day in April, Grover went outside to answer the call of nature and collapsed. When Claire rushed to his aid he fixed her with a look.

She knew what that look meant. She had seen it in his eyes the first day she met him five years earlier.

It said, *Help me, please.*

Grover chose Claire because he knew he could trust her to care for him. He knew she would love him and treat him with kindness and always act in his best interest. That was what he was asking her to do now.

'We called the vet around and they said, "Yes, it doesn't get better from here, it only gets worse."'

It ripped her heart in two, but she knew she had to let her best boy go. 'It was the hardest thing for us, but we knew it was the kindest thing for Grover.'

Grover's passing left an enormous hole in Claire's life, but she will forever be grateful that he is immortalised in the books he inspired. To this day, more than six years after the first Grover McBane: Rescue Dog book was published, she still receives messages from children that have just read their first Grover tale.

'There are not many dogs whose lives have been enshrined on bookshelves around the world. I'm so glad that I wrote the books about him,' says Claire. 'I had this perfect alignment of passion and idea and inspiration that all came to me at the same time. It was such a unique experience and I just feel honoured that I got to share it with him.'

Claire has since moved on from the SDCH but will always have a soft spot in her heart for the place that brought Grover into her life. She has another much-loved border collie, too – but Grover will forever be the dog who taught her about friendship, resilience and living every day to the full.

'We just always knew he was magic,' she says.

That's the real reason Grover chose Claire: to make her believe in magic.

Mumma Zura

The Staffy supermum

The list of mothers of that have raised the most children makes for fascinating reading. The all-time record is held by the wife of Russian peasant Feodor Vassilyev – some sources say her name was Valentina, while others don't bother giving her a name at all. She is said to have given birth to an astonishing sixty-nine children, with the last child born around 1765.

The Vassilyev brood reputedly included sixteen pairs of twins, seven sets of triplets and four sets of quadruplets. Feodor supposedly also had a further eighteen children with his second wife.

In modern times, Ugandan woman Mariam Nabatanzi had delivered forty-four children by her thirty-sixth birthday in 2016. Her prolific reproduction was caused by a rare genetic condition that caused hyperovulation – after welcoming three sets of quadruplets, four sets of triplets and six pairs of twins, in 2019 Mariam had surgery to prevent further pregnancies.

But it isn't giving birth that makes somebody a mother. Stepmothers, adoptive and foster mothers, women whose children were born via surrogacy and trans women are all mums. There are women all over the world that have loved and nurtured vastly more offspring than they delivered themselves.

Adelaide-born Geraldine Cox doesn't have biological children, but more than a thousand children have called her 'Big Mamma' since she opened her first orphanage in Cambodia in the nineties. English mum-of-three Birdie McDonald fostered more than 850 children in her London home; she signed up as a carer in 1975 and continued for more than forty years.

Mothering isn't the sole preserve of human beings, of course. Females of every species produce offspring (and some males, too – looking at you, seahorses), but raising young that are not biologically their own is also common in the animal kingdom.

Scientists working with gorillas in Rwanda have observed the primates banding together to take care of orphans, while bonobo apes have been known to adopt babies from different social groups. Sometimes animals even take it upon themselves to raise other species, like the bottlenose dolphin who 'fostered' a melon-headed whale calf in French Polynesia in 2019, or the wild capuchin monkeys that brought up a baby marmoset in 2004.

All of which is to say that the definition of a mother is an expansive and amorphous thing. In fact, there is really only one thing mums tend to have in common: a limitless capacity for love.

That's something that Mumma Zura the American Staffordshire terrier had in spades, both in terms of the love she received from her doting dads – Chris Melotti and Scott Banning – and the love she doled out to the 'kids' in her care.

Chris has loved dogs all his life. His first pooch was the family dog, a 'gorgeous' Pomeranian called Jack who was there for most of his childhood.

Next came Toby the beagle, a dog so special that his early passing devastated the Melotti family. 'Toby was a beautiful boy and cherished by my family, especially my dad, who still talks about him to this day,' says Chris. 'Sadly, he was diagnosed with cancer when he was only seven and passed away just a few weeks later. It was a very big shock to my family. I have two siblings, and all three of us grew up and moved out, but my parents still can't bring themselves to get another dog.'

Chris met his husband Scott in 2015, and they soon decided they were ready for a dog of their own. They knew they wanted to rescue their new four-legged family member from a shelter. Trouble was, they couldn't decide which dog to adopt.

'We went to a Sydney shelter a few times, because we just couldn't make a decision. We were looking and looking and looking, and we went back three times,' says Chris.

On the couple's third visit, the decision was made for them when shelter staff offered an unexpected solution. They revealed they had recently confiscated a litter of American Staffordshire terriers that were not yet out in the public viewing area. Would they like to meet one?

The pup staff had in mind was a six-week-old Staffy with a striking blue-grey coat. Chris and Scott were instantly smitten and decided to name her Zura, a short-ened version of azzurra, the Italian word for the colour sky blue. The name was actually suggested by Chris's mum.

It can also be an adaptation of the Persian word for 'strength', which would prove to be a prescient choice for Zura. 'The name just fit her so well. She was very bold and motherly, but also quite strict,' says Chris.

Being surrounded by love wasn't always the norm for Zura. The first few weeks of her life are something of a mystery, but it is thought to have involved neglect at best and outright cruelty at worst.

'It was never confirmed, but the staff alluded to the fact that Zura had been bred for dog fighting,' Chris explains. 'She definitely had the right physique for that. She was very lean and tall and muscular, but not stocky. She was a lovely little thing, very pretty.'

Chris and Scott knew the moment they met her that Zura would be coming home with them. This was the reason they had struggled to find the right dog to adopt: they were waiting for her.

Zura settled into her new life as though she had always been there. Chris and Scott were amazed that she didn't seem to be burdened by whatever she had endured in her early life. She wasn't anxious or fearful, and she didn't have any physical scars or injuries. She was just a happy, goofy and loving dog, not to mention incredibly intelligent. 'A real alpha dog,' says Chris.

The couple have encountered some shocking cases of cruelty to dogs in the years since, which make Zura's well-adjusted temperament seem even more remarkable.

'We've had some really tricky cases – dogs that were on four different anti-anxiety drugs three times a day, that sort of thing. Zura didn't show signs of any of that,' says Chris.

Chris and Scott adopted Zura in November 2015. In early 2017, they decided Zura needed a friend. 'Scott thought she was a little bit lonely and said, "Let's get another dog,"' says Chris.

They were renting at that time and Chris wasn't sure whether their lease permitted two dogs. He suggested a compromise. They'd had such a positive experience adopting Zura – why not foster a dog this time, to give her some company and road test being a two-dog family?

'We were moving around and I wasn't sure what we could and couldn't have, so I said, "Let's just do some fostering so we can meet some dogs and see how it all goes,"' he says.

Famous last words.

When Chris and Scott brought their first litter of foster puppies home from the same Sydney shelter that October, it was with some trepidation. Zura had never been anything other than lovely towards other animals she met, but this was different. They were bringing new dogs into her home; dogs that would require time-consuming care and attention. Would she put up with having to share her dads' affection? Would she accept these interlopers when they were on her turf?

As it turned out, she would not.

She would not *just* accept the foster pups, that is. She wouldn't *merely* tolerate them. Instead, Zura fell head-over-heels in love with each and every one of them. She nurtured and protected them as if they were her own offspring. And she would do it over and over and over again.

This was the beginning of *many* beautiful friendships.

Dogs are like potato chips: it's almost impossible to stop at just one.

Chris and Scott definitely feel that way and, when they started fostering puppies, it became clear that Zura did too.

After that first litter of wriggling little fuzzballs they fostered, Zura simply could not get enough. Virtually overnight, she morphed into a supermum.

'She just took to it immediately. I've never seen such a motherly dog. She was desexed when she came to us, so she'd never had her own puppies, but she would play with them and look after them,' says Chris. 'We started fostering to give back and be the yin to that yang that dogs go through, and it was like she knew. It was a beautiful thing to watch.'

Though they had initially decided to foster puppies in the hope of finding a second dog to adopt, Chris and Scott found the experience so rewarding that they decided to become ongoing foster carers instead.

And so that first litter of pups was followed by another . . . and another. The novelty of new arrivals never wore off – not for Chris and Scott, and certainly not for Zura.

'I would feel a thrill every time we brought puppies home because I knew how excited Zura would be,' he says. 'We'd put down the pet carrier and all the dogs would spill out, and her tail would be going wild. She'd be all over them.'

Her natural maternal instinct quickly earned her the nickname 'Mumma Zura' among staff at the shelter she'd come from. She became the go-to girl for puppies that needed the guiding hand of a mother that, for one reason or another, they were growing up without.

Though she was patient and kind, Zura wouldn't hesitate to correct the pups when their behaviour became a little unruly – just as their biological mothers would have.

'She taught them how to go to the toilet, when to eat, what to eat. She could be quite stern when she needed to be. She was never aggressive, but she would huff to bring them into line,' says Chris. 'We had two huskies once that were all over her, and she never got angry.'

Puppies came to Chris and Scott for a range of reasons. Some were sick or weak, while others were anxious and found the shelter environment too stressful. Some had been abused and were involved in court cases. Their breeds ranged from large (huskies and other Staffies) to pint-sized (poodles and terriers); Zura was even foster mum to four kittens and Sebastian, an albino Staffy who was born deaf.

She seemed to instinctively understand that some of the puppies were fragile and she needed to be extra gentle around them.

'What really spins me out is that she wasn't even very old when we started fostering. It was fascinating how she knew not to do certain things. She never stood on them, ever, even though they were always underfoot,' Chris says. 'She would play tug-of-war with them, and I know from playing with her myself that she had some strength. She could have flung them right over the neighbours' fence because they were so small, but she knew exactly the amount of strength to use. She would growl in a playful way, but she would never yank them or throw them.'

Thanks to Zura's exemplary mothering skills, shelter staff asked Chris and Scott whether they would be willing to undertake additional training that would equip them to take on foster pups with more complex needs.

They immediately agreed. With Zura on their team, they knew they could handle anything.

'They would give us what they call the "witness protection" cases – dogs that couldn't be shared on social media and couldn't be on view in the shelter,' Chris explains. 'Zura was given some really difficult cases, but she was so good with them. It just shows how special she was.'

She was so committed to 'her' puppies that Zura fretted when they were out of her sight for even a few moments.

'There was one time when we went away for the weekend and gave Zura and the foster puppies to my parents. We put Zura in the car first and then went to get the puppies,' he says. 'She was hesitant to get in because she knew the puppies weren't there yet. Even my mum noticed.'

With Zura's help, all the foster puppies grew into healthy, happy dogs. Crucially, they also learned that humans could be trusted. Zura had not only shown them how to 'dog', she had also modelled a healthy canine–human bond for them.

Chris says that even puppies that were only a few weeks old sometimes exhibited fear of people when they first arrived. 'There were a few cases where we would go to gently discipline a puppy and it would flinch as if to say, *Don't hit me*. Thanks to Zura we were able to reinforce that humans were safe and could be a happy place for the dogs.'

Zura loved all of her charges equally, never showing favourites. 'I never saw that. If we had three puppies, she just had a natural instinct for looking after them quite equally. The way I would describe it is she would just mother them all. She'd be there on her bed and they would all be lying there with her.'

In the end, Scott chose a favourite for her in June 2019. Olympia was a mix of French mastiff and Dogue de Bordeaux, both giant breeds, and even at just twelve weeks old she was enormous. She had arrived in foster care with a broken leg, and she grew at such a rapid rate that Chris and Scott had to have her cast changed every week.

When Scott confessed that he wanted to keep Olympia, Chris was initially unsure. They were still renting, and they already had four-year-old Zura and up to five other pups on any given day. Plus, she was just so *big*.

'Even the shelter staff said, "Are you sure? She's so big!" But Scott said, "We've got the space and we've got the love." Eventually I caved and we never looked back.'

Call it mother's intuition, but Zura seemed to know that Olympia was staying right from the off. She bonded with her in a way she never did with the other foster dogs.

'Olympia and Zura were besties straight away. They were just inseparable,' he says.

Chris and Scott are often asked how they can bear to say goodbye to their foster puppies when the time comes for them to go to their forever homes. In this, they have always followed the example Zura set.

'People will say, "How do you give them up?" and we say, "That's just how it works." Zura always accepted the dogs she got. It didn't matter how long she had with them, she had the same attitude: *They're off now, and there will be new ones to come.*

'We were worried that she would get depressed, because she did get very attached to them, and we knew that mother dogs could mope when they were separated from their puppies, but never once did she get sad. She was always like, *Now I'm waiting for the next one.*'

In fact, there were times that Zura seemed to breathe a big sigh of relief when the latest litter went on its merry way. Even the most devoted mother needs a break every now and then.

'Sometimes we would have a puppy for months on end and it could be quite a challenge. When they left, Zura would often be like, *Thank gosh, now we get a break*,' Chris says with a chuckle. 'The shelter would ask us if we would take another one and we'd give Zura a few weeks of breathing space. But then she would want another dog, so we'd get one for her. That was what she needed.'

By 2020, Zura had mothered more than 200 foster dogs. That year, she was a finalist in the foster-care story category of the Pet Insurance Australia Companion Animal Rescue Awards. She didn't win the category, but instead received her very own honour: the Drontal Special Foster Carer Award.

Chris and Scott could not have been prouder of their beautiful girl.

'We got this reputation for being great foster carers, but it was Zura who was doing all the work,' says Chris. 'It was Zura who really loved them and nurtured them all back to health.'

They hoped that Zura would show Olympia the ropes of foster parenting, so that she could share the load and even take over Zura's den mother role someday, but Olympia doesn't have the same interest in puppies.

'Olympia is one of those dogs who has so much personality without even trying. She's just fascinating. She's quite the specimen,' he says. 'She will tolerate the foster dogs but it will take her a while to warm up to them, and with Zura it never did.'

That's because Zura was quite simply one of a kind. Perhaps she threw herself into mothering her fostered brood with such enthusiasm because she knew her time here would be short.

Zura had always been plagued by more serious medical problems than any dog should ever have to endure. She had ruptured her anterior cruciate ligament and survived fluid on the lungs, among other ailments. By the time she was five years old she'd had five major surgeries, including an invasive procedure to relieve compression on her spinal cord.

Chris estimates he and Scott spent $30,000 on Zura's surgeries and ongoing veterinary treatment, but nothing was able to procure the lasting good health she so deserved.

'She just had problem after problem after problem. I suspect it was a result of backyard breeding. It was like she was cursed, but she was a fighter and we tried everything,' he says. 'The vets would say, "This surgery is going to have an eight-week hospital recovery," but then call us days after the operation to say she was doing so well she could come home. She was pretty incredible.'

But in 2021, when she was just five years old, Zura suddenly began to cough up blood. Chris and Scott rushed her to the vet and she rallied, but a few days later she was struggling to breathe again. This heartbreaking cycle continued until the couple realised they couldn't let their adored dog continue to suffer.

'Every day there was something new. Her body was just constantly breaking down. It got to the point where we said, "Where do we draw the line? We can't keep doing this to this poor dog."'

They made the devastating decision to let Zura go on 8 October 2021.

'It was a horrible decision to have to make, but we tried to think of it as the final gift that we were able to give her.'

Chris and Scott had promised to give Zura a lifetime of love and happiness. They kept that promise – it was just that her lifetime was far, far too short.

For a while they wondered whether they should continue to foster dogs. But how could they possibly do it without Zura, especially when Olympia had never been overly keen on the arrangement?

They got their answer later in 2021, when they brought home Rosco the Labrador. While he's not the same tireless parent that Zura was – she was truly something special – he is wonderful with the foster pups in his own special way.

'He's a typical Lab: anything and everything gets love. He plays the same sort of role that Zura did. He comes in and bridges that gap between Olympia and the foster puppies,' Chris says. 'He will play with the new dogs, and Olympia will play with him, but she won't want to play with the new dogs, so he gets sandwiched between Olympia and every new arrival. The poor thing just gets nipped and grabbed at both ends!'

With Rosco in the team, Chris and Scott are committed to fostering for as long as possible.

'We just love it. It's a nice experience and we really enjoy being a part of it, getting involved and being a force for good.'

And while they love fostering, they also love the idea of carrying on Zura's important work. She has left such a legacy that there is now a plaque dedicated to her in the memorial garden at the shelter where her story began.

Most dog owners believe their pets are one of a kind, but Chris hopes that's *not* true in Zura's case. In a perfect world, he says, there would be many, many more dogs just like her: nurturing, full of love, and always ready to step up and help those in need.

'As unique as she was, I hope that there's a lot more of her out there. I hope that she wasn't rare,' he says. 'I would hate to think that kind of love existed only for the fleeting five years that *she* existed. I hope that it didn't die with her. She was so special to us. She made life enjoyable and much more colourful, and she was just such a good dog. She was a matriarch and I miss that. She kept the whole house in order.'

Just like any good mum.

Frankie

The walking explorer

By his own admission, Benjamin 'Benny' Scott is not the sort of man to do anything by halves. When he decides to do something, Benny really *does* it. He's 100 per cent committed, all or nothing, go big or go home.

A lot of the time, it's a wonderful approach to life. Benny has squeezed more experiences and adventures into his twenty-nine years than many people manage in a lifetime.

But it can also be a destructive personality trait – something Benny knows all too well. He loves hard and works hard, but for a long time he played even harder. He threw himself into a dangerous lifestyle with his trademark intensity and focus, and it nearly cost him everything.

'That's my personality: everything is intense. I can't focus on anything until something really grabs me, and then I can't take my mind off that. When something really grips me, I'll always stick with it,' he says.

This attitude is no doubt what took Benny to China in 2015, when he was twenty-one.

'I've always done out-of-the-box sort of stuff. I was at kind of a loose end and needed a change, so I was looking for expat work overseas.'

His mother, Tamara, is German, but he had never learned the language. He decided that he had missed an opportunity.

'I grew up with a multicultural background, but I was never patient enough to learn German. So I thought it would be good to learn Chinese,' Benny explains. 'I'd been partying and getting into small trouble, so going overseas was my own little recovery. A way of trying to grow as a person without going to university – because I wasn't a uni boy.'

He moved to the sprawling industrial city of Fuzhou, the capital and one of the biggest cities in China's Fujian province, where he had landed a job teaching English at a training school. Also known as training centres, these private academies tutor students between three and twelve years old in subjects such as English, maths, or Chinese. They operate outside of normal school hours, usually in the evenings and on weekends.

Benny threw himself into his new life with typical enthusiasm. 'Because I went to China to learn Mandarin Chinese, I made a conscious decision to not have foreigner friends. I only had Chinese friends,' he says.

In the end, Benny lived in China for five years. 'I was

only going to go for a year, but after a year I hadn't learned squat, so I thought, *I guess I'm staying.*'

He did soon gain a good grasp of the language – many people in Fuzhou speak a specific Fuzhou dialect as well as Mandarin Chinese – and used it to set up a couple of 'side hustle' ventures to supplement his part-time teaching income.

'I tried a few business things, like selling vitamins and baby formula. But that was a really hard market to break into,' he says.

The business idea that took off was an organic evolution of the work he was already doing. He had gotten to know the parents of some of his students by practising Chinese with them after class. Soon they were inquiring about extra tutoring for their children, so he took the plunge and opened his own private tuition business.

'I got some flyers printed and turned the lounge room of my apartment into a classroom. Soon I had up to fifty kids turning up,' says Benny. 'Running the business really helped my Chinese. I was constantly liaising with the parents, because they'd want to know how their kids were doing.'

By that time, Benny felt like a full-fledged Fuzhou resident. He had a Chinese girlfriend and travelled everywhere on his motor scooter. A lifelong dog lover, he also rescued a Fuzhou street dog – but he soon realised he was not the owner the dog deserved.

'I adopted him for the long term, but I signed up for more than I could handle. It wasn't like having a dog in

Australia. I was in a very small apartment and sometimes working twelve-hour days,' says Benny. 'He was a puppy and I had nowhere to walk him.'

After three weeks, he felt the best thing for the pup was to return him to the rescue group so he could find an owner whose lifestyle was better suited to dog ownership.

It was fortuitous timing, because not long afterwards Benny's life in China came to an abrupt end. He suffered a very minor injury in a scooter accident in November 2019, but it quickly turned out to be a *major* problem.

'It was wet outside and I was riding on the footpath, and there was a film of mud over it. I was doing about thirty kilometres per hour and I slid – the wheels went out from underneath me and I hit the dirt. It was like skiing. I didn't even hit the brakes,' he says. 'But I only had a small graze on my ankle. I just picked the bike up and went home.'

By the next morning, however, Benny knew something was very wrong. The grazed foot had swelled up 'like a football' and was obviously infected. He went to the doctor for a course of antibiotics, but they were powerless against the infection.

'I had a metal plate in my ankle from a previous injury when I was a kid, and because of that it was quite easy for the infection to move up into the bone,' he explains.

Within days, necrosis and gangrene developed in Benny's foot; the tissue was literally dying due to a lack of blood supply. Left untreated, gangrene can be fatal within forty-eight hours.

Benny got straight on a plane back to Australia.

'I landed at the airport in Sydney and went straight from the arrivals hall to the hospital. Within twenty-four hours I was in surgery to cut out the necrosis and gangrene.'

He was in hospital for a month, and the full recovery from his frightening ordeal took several more weeks. But Benny was enjoying being back in his home country, with his family and friends around him. He had already been thinking about returning home before his accident, so while a life-threatening emergency wasn't quite the homecoming he'd anticipated, he was happy to be in back Sydney.

Still, he expected to return to Fuzhou when he was well enough – if for no other reason than to wind up his business and have a proper farewell with his friends there.

'I had this business that was taking off, but I didn't want to teach anymore. I think I was in a bit of denial. I had never planned to stay in China for such a long time, so the accident helped to close that chapter faster,' he concedes. 'Then the COVID-19 pandemic hit. There was no chance of going back. It ended up costing me a lot of money, because of the abruptness of it. I didn't get much closure over there.'

Once he was – literally – back on his own two feet, Benny did exactly what he'd done in China: he dived headfirst into his new life. He moved in with a friend who worked as a chef and adopted his hard-partying lifestyle, which involved lots of late nights and recreational drugs.

Around the same time, Benny began a new relationship with a woman who was also partial to chemically enhancing a night out. The heady combination of new love, chemical highs and Benny's admittedly full-throttle personality was a recipe for disaster. Almost before he knew it, Benny was in the grip of full-blown cocaine and cannabis addiction.

He used drugs for about a year before realising his habit was out of control. Then he spent another year trying to stop, but each short-lived period of sobriety would be followed by another drug binge.

'My then girlfriend could sustain a job, keep a straight head, and keep her life somewhat together, but my using was completely unsustainable. It got really, really dark there sometimes, really bad psychosis,' Benny says. 'I knew what I was doing. I knew it was wrong and I didn't want to be doing it, because it was ruining my life, but I'd want that instant high. I'd get sober and then two weeks later go back to using massive amounts of cocaine because I hadn't built enough of a life to keep me sober. It's so complex.'

Benny had moved in with his girlfriend, and they soon decided to get a dog together. He knew immediately that he wanted a German shepherd. Perhaps it's his self-confessed tendency towards single-minded focus that explains why Benny feels such an affinity with the tenacious breed. Originally bred as herding dogs at the turn of the nineteenth century, German shepherds are dogs that need a purpose. They are naturally curious and eager to learn, which means they can be stubborn once they get an idea in their heads. Sound familiar?

Benny got to know the breed early on thanks to his German grandmother, who had them all her life. His mum, Tamara, also had German shepherds when Benny was growing up at Crescent Head on the New South Wales north coast. His own childhood dogs were kelpies and a much-loved Maremma sheepdog–kelpie mix called Grommet.

'I love German shepherds because they're so intelligent and so loyal,' he says.

So, in November 2020, Benny and his partner visited a breeder. They chose an adorable fuzzy puppy and named him Frankie. Benny hoped he would help him in his quest to conquer his drug habit. It was arguably not the best reason to get a dog, but Benny's love for his new four-legged friend was pure, and his care unimpeachable.

'Getting Frankie was part of a process to keep us sober, but unfortunately for the first half year of his life, or more, he had addicted parents,' he says. 'But I'm a dog person, and he'd get me outside to go to the park once or twice a day. He gave me a sense of responsibility and accountability. But living in the city, living that same life, the grip of addiction was still there. Frankie helped us take a lot less, but we were still taking.'

Benny's frustration at his apparent inability to stop using cocaine was growing by the day. If he couldn't do it for Frankie, what was it going to take? He was almost afraid of the answer.

But he got it anyway, in the form of a sharp wake-up call from a friend.

'We had a roommate living with us in the spare bedroom. He was a close friend of mine and had been through his own recovery journey. He saw me one day and said, "If you don't die this weekend, you need to change your whole life right now,"' he recalls.

Somehow, his friend's words struck a chord with Benny. Other people in his life had pleaded with him to seek help, but their appeals largely fell on deaf ears. He did consider checking himself into a rehabilitation facility, but he couldn't find any that were pet friendly. He wasn't willing to leave Frankie behind.

Hearing it from someone who had been down in the depths themselves, however, hit differently.

'Even my girlfriend had tried, but she was also using, and an addict can't get an addict to stop,' he says. 'But when my friend told me to stop, it really resonated deep within.'

In an instant, Benny understood that his drug use was completely out of control. He wasn't the sort of person who could use just a little bit, or only occasionally; he would take drugs until he reached oblivion.

And he couldn't stop by himself, either. He had tried that again and again, but even his best mate Frankie couldn't keep him on the straight and narrow. He would have to ask for help.

'I tried and tried. I kept saying to myself, "If I just do a little bit, it's okay," but I finally got the picture that if I did it once, I was doing it all,' he says. 'I could not control the habit.'

His roommate put Benny in touch with a chaplain who had been a big help with his own recovery. When Benny called the man, he didn't mince words. 'He said, "If it was up to me, I'd take you to hospital. You need to change." I knew I couldn't do it myself, so I decided to do everything he said.'

Once he'd made the decision to choose sobriety, Benny didn't think twice. As is his way, it was full steam ahead. Benny ended his relationship, packed his belongings, and he and Frankie went back to the family home at Crescent Head.

It was an enormous, painful wrench – but he had to do it. He felt his life literally depended on it.

'I just went into full action mode,' he says.

As the fog of his addiction started to dissipate, a newly clear-headed Benny had the time and mental space to contemplate what he wanted his new, sober life to look like. He knew he needed a focus, some outlet for his relentless energy. The risks of floating around without a project to anchor him were too great.

For several years Benny had harboured a dream to undertake some sort of extreme physical challenge. For a while he considered a cross-continental skateboarding trip in India, but the condition of the roads there quickly scuppered that idea. Then he remembered a YouTube video he'd seen about a man who'd circumnavigated the globe with his dog. At the time, he had filed the idea away in his mental 'cool ideas for the future' folder.

It appeared the future was now.

No sooner had the idea come back to him than Benny 'was like a bull at a gate' with the project. He would walk around the world to raise awareness of addiction and mental health, and he would take Frankie with him.

'Within a week of getting sober, I was trying to do this. It was a real 180-degree flip. I wanted to do something "out there", partly to test my mettle. I wanted to do the hardest of the hard,' he says. 'I've always been an extreme person, and walking is so mundane that I had to make it extreme.'

It was time to start walking the long road to lasting recovery.

Years earlier, Benny had 'soft launched' his plan to walk the globe by casually floating the idea among his friends and family. But when he made the official announcement in November 2021 that he was actually, really, *truly* going to do it, he encountered plenty of scepticism.

'Over the years I would say, "I'm going to do this," and see what people thought. My family and friends were very sceptical. They were like, *Here we go again.* They thought the same thing as when I went to China,' he says. 'It was understandable. There's been a million projects before that I haven't finished or have got bored with.'

This time, however, Benny just knew he would complete his mission. He spent six months planning and preparing for his expedition on a full-time basis.

The first step was mapping out the route he would take. He decided that he and Frankie would first walk from Sydney to Darwin, then trek to Bangkok and Beijing, then head north-east and ultimately end their epic journey in Alaska.

'I really just looked at the map. Alaska is my sister's name, so making it there represented making it home, making it back to family.'

The route would require Benny and Frankie to cross the Bering Sea, something only a handful of man-and-dog teams had ever achieved.

'I wanted to do the most extreme route that was possible,' he says with a laugh.

Next, Benny needed to get his gear together. Fortunately, he already had a blueprint for the supplies he would need, thanks to Tom Turcich. Tom, a 33-year-old American who hails from New Jersey, spent seven years circumnavigating the globe on foot after the death of a close friend when they were both teenagers. That experience had inspired him to live every day to the fullest.

Four months into his journey, Tom adopted a rescue pup, Savannah, from a Texas shelter. His original plan hadn't included a walking buddy, but when he found himself struggling to sleep at campsites, he thought having a watchdog would help him get some much-needed rest.

When Tom and Savannah completed their 45,000-kilometre circumnavigation in New Jersey, on 21 May 2022, he became only the tenth person to circle the planet on foot. Savannah went into the history books as the first dog to do it.

Tom had charted his journey on Instagram, Facebook and YouTube, where he has a combined 148,000 followers – including Benny.

'I watched every single video Tom had on YouTube – everything he takes, his kit, how to get visas for dogs. I started to replicate his kit, and to this day it's very similar,' he says. 'Tom uses a Thule Chariot baby pram to carry his gear and that's the one I've got.'

Benny also taught himself the basics of video editing and learned what kind of equipment he would need to post updates from the road.

When Benny first decided to walk around the world, he thought he would partner with an existing charity – but the chaplain who was guiding him in his recovery efforts offered a better idea. 'He's actually super business savvy, and he was telling me to start my own charity. He helped me get a lawyer and write up a constitution,' he says.

That's how Benny's charity, Walk2Recovery, was born.

Next, Benny emailed 'every single person I could think of who might give me a discount on some gear'. Every little bit of progress he made towards his goal felt like another step on the road to recovery, and he hadn't even begun walking yet.

'I knew I was going to do this to get sober, but it was a dream well before then. I bought a tent online months before I really started planning for the trip,' he says. 'Gradually it became a real thing. I did my first video, which was an introduction to me and Frankie and what we were doing. I did all the paperwork for the charity. I developed a daily routine in recovery before I even set out on the journey.'

He also secured a major sponsor, Sherpa, an Australian-owned supplier of outdoor clothing and equipment. 'They gave me everything at cost price, so I was able to upgrade from my fifty-dollar eBay tent to a proper tent.'

Soon enough, the only thing left to do was to actually start walking. On 29 December 2021, he and Frankie set off for Darwin from the iconic, hertitage-listed *I Have a Dream* mural in the Sydney suburb of Newtown. They walked around 35 kilometres, to the outer western suburbs, with all their worldly goods packed into a baby's pram.

On one hand that first day felt like a watershed moment after months of planning. On the other, it felt like it didn't really count. Family and friends accompanied the intrepid man and dog for that entire first stint; it wasn't until the next day that they were truly on their own.

'When I gave my parents and my family a hug and said goodbye on day two, that felt like, *I'm really doing it now. It was just a feeling of adventure. I'm walking away from my old life and into my new life.*'

An amazing discovery not long before they left gave Benny added confidence that he was meant to do this journey – that the universe was on his side.

Benny's father, Hugh, is adopted. He had spent the better part of a decade searching for members of his biological family. Just a week before Benny set off, Hugh finally made contact with his brother and two sisters.

Incredibly, it turns out his sister, Paula Constant, is also an extreme long-distance walker. Between 2004 and 2007, she travelled 12,500 kilometres on foot through eight countries. For 7000 kilometres of that journey she walked solo with a camel train across the Sahara. Paula detailed her adventures in two books, *Long Journey South* and *Sahara*.

(There were further uncanny coincidences: Hugh and Tamara live on a boat; Hugh's brother is a yacht skipper and their biological father spent the last years of his life sailing. His name, astonishingly, was Frank.)

'We knew intuitively that this was the right thing to be doing, but finding out all that was like the icing on the cake,' says Benny.

From the day they set off, Benny and Frankie were dogged – pun intended – about their progress. On average they walked a cycle of four days on and three days off, so they could rest and Benny could edit and upload social media posts and YouTube videos. On their walking days they usually covered around 40 kilometres – sometimes more, sometimes less.

They once did a 24-hour non-stop challenge, in which they covered 100 kilometres. Benny walked the entire time, while Frankie had frequent rests and naps in the pram. They followed that with a week off.

'There were times we'd do twenty-five kilometres a day and really relax through it, but most of the time I'd rush a bit to get to the next town so I'd have more time to rest,' says Benny. 'If I wasn't full of energy, I didn't keep going. It was a really spontaneous journey the whole way. The plan would change and we would change with it.'

The pair camped most nights, sleeping in their tent or on a tarpaulin under the stars if it was warm enough, but they availed themselves of small-town motels and caravan parks when they could. They almost always awoke before sunrise and started walking at first light.

'I always liked to start walking before I'd eaten, even if it was just half an hour. But I would feed Frankie early so he could have half an hour to digest his food while I was packing up,' Benny says.

Weather was always an important consideration. On one memorable occasion, Benny and Frankie were trapped inside their tent by bad weather for thirty hours. But it was walking through the outback in the middle of summer that proved one of the biggest early challenges.

'We were walking differently every day. We'd walk to the weather and we'd walk to how we felt. Sometimes I would follow my watch and we'd walk in two-hour blocks. Sometimes I'd just follow my nose,' he says. 'If we were on a treeless plain, we'd hardly stop at all – it's hotter to stop, because when you're walking you've got the breeze.'

Through the entire journey, Frankie's comfort and wellbeing was always Benny's top priority. He pushed the 37-kilogram dog in the pram whenever he needed to rest, and made sure he walked on grass rather than bitumen as much as possible to protect his paws. He even tried special dog booties, but they caused Frankie's dew claws to chafe, so he did away with that idea.

There were a couple of times early on in the expedition, when they were still figuring out a daily routine that worked for them, where Benny concedes he pushed his stoic companion a little too far.

'There was a time there when it was really hot and it was always a battle. Even in the shade, I could tell Frankie was uncomfortably hot. I always carried ice packs and would put them on him,' says Benny. 'He chased a kangaroo once at midday in the middle of summer when it was thirty-nine degrees. I had to drench him in water and put an ice pack on him to cool him down.'

But there is no doubt that Frankie was absolutely living his best life out on the open road. He was with his best friend 24/7, and any time they encountered other people he received a steady stream of treats and cuddles.

'He adapted so well over time, and I adapted as well. You should have seen how excited he would be to get moving again. He would get sick of the downtime and want to get going, especially when the weather got cooler,' Benny says.

Such an ambitious adventure was never going to be sunshine and happiness every moment of every day – not for Frankie and not for him. Benny knew from the outset that there would inevitably be bad days. He was, after all, trying to walk 4000 kilometres with his dog *and* maintain his recovery from addiction at the same time. As well as the weight of his gear, he carried a heavy mental load on his shoulders.

But having Frankie by his side made the dark days infinitely easier.

'The best part about doing it with Frankie was the companionship. I was down deep, head in my hands, and he pulled me out of the depths. And it was an equally tough journey for him as it was for me. I'm not going to sugarcoat it,' he says. 'Anything really good can get really bad, too, but any time I felt that way he would come and nuzzle his way in and almost slap me out of that thought process. He did that so many times. He just really made me laugh it off and get up and keep moving. I couldn't have gone that far without him.'

Keep moving they did – for six months. After 4073 kilometres and exactly 180 days on the road, Benny and Frankie arrived in Darwin on the afternoon of 27 June 2022. Benny's parents had flown in to meet him, and the dauntless explorers were greeted by a round of applause at the iconic Mindil Beach.

Benny immediately took off his shoes, and he and Frankie ceremonially dunked their pram's front wheel in the ocean. Then Benny ate an enormous hamburger while Frankie received a full veterinary check-up – he was given a clean bill of health.

'I was completely taken back by how much support was shown. Literally hundreds of cars beeping and people shouting out the windows, and cars stopping to show support, really felt like a homecoming far away from home,' Benny wrote on Instagram the next day. 'I woke up feeling grateful but slightly lost in the sense that I didn't have to pack up my kit and start walking. This journey has changed me in so many ways. And I am happy to say it is a blessing to wake up and put clean socks and undies on!'

Benny and Frankie spent a little over a fortnight in Darwin, resting and reacclimatising to 'normal' life.

(This took a little longer for Frankie, who 'thinks everything that moves that isn't human is a rabbit, pig or lizard that must be chased'.)

Never able to sit still for long, however, Benny's mind quickly turned to the next phase of his and Frankie's epic journey. He revised his original plan and decided to travel on to Perth instead of Asia, this time by car, so that he could work for a while and save some money for the next phase.

Beyond that, who knows? Benny is still sober and remains focused on building his charity, Walk2Recovery. His ultimate goal is to build a pet-friendly recovery centre.

Life could take him anywhere, but one thing is sure: wherever Benny goes, Frankie will be by his side every step of the way.

Yale

The wellbeing wonderdog

We often hear that children are naturally resilient. And it is true that many little people seem to have some built-in capacity for bouncing back from challenges and tough times, recovering from setbacks and getting back to living life.

But while it's great that kids *can* overcome serious hardship, it's sad that so many of them have to. In a perfect world, young people would never be burdened by anxiety or fear. They wouldn't have to soldier on through stress and uncertainty. They'd have no need to develop the skills necessary to cope with trauma.

Kids' top priorities in life should include making friends, exploring the world around them, and finding the fun in every situation. Instead, 21st-century children are bombarded by frightening news headlines and forced to try to make sense of a world that feels scary and overwhelming.

That has never been truer than in the past few years, with the COVID-19 pandemic disrupting every aspect of life for kids and adults alike. Babies born during the pandemic have reportedly been slower to form friendships with other kids, because for the first formative years of their lives they were in isolation. Meanwhile, multiple lockdowns across most Australian states between 2020 and 2022 meant school moved online for the majority of students. Suddenly, they couldn't run around in the playground, and they could only see their teachers and friends through a computer screen.

(Unsurprisingly, hours of screen time shot up while activity levels plummeted. According to research from Deakin University's Institute for Physical Activity and Nutrition, during the 2020 lockdowns children spent almost 27 more hours on their screens each week.)

Teachers truly went above and beyond to try to make remote learning as interactive and engaging as possible, but it just wasn't the same as being in the classroom. It was nobody's fault – nobody but the virus, anyway – but children's wellbeing declined. The longer they were away, the more their worries about school and friendships increased.

And so did their anxiety about what school would be like when they finally *were* allowed to go back.

The eventual return to face-to-face schooling was always going to be a tricky thing for kids to navigate. Cathy Hey is the principal of Trinity Catholic Primary

School at Kemps Creek in the western suburbs of Sydney, and she realised this well before students pulled on their backpacks for their first day back at school.

Cathy is an educator with more than thirty-one years' experience and she is well versed in the workings of young minds. She knew her students would be nervous and worried about returning to school, so she started thinking about ways to make that transition easier.

Trinity has long had a strong focus on its students' wellbeing, and on connection throughout the school community. The K–6 school offers voluntary mindfulness activities, including lunchtime meditation, gardening and dance clubs, and it has a creative makerspace in which children are encouraged to 'design, engineer, fabricate, build, create, tinker and collaborate' to their hearts' content.

Every Friday from noon, Cathy sits in the school's courtyard and invites students to share their good news with her in an event she calls Happy Hour. It is enormously popular with students and was much-missed during lockdowns.

'It could be that they've lost their first tooth or scored a goal at netball, or it could be a school-based achievement,' she says. 'Our school is always a happy, positive place. I say to the kids every day, "Kind thoughts, kind words, kind actions." We see it all around the school.'

And every school morning from eight o'clock, Cathy is stationed in the car park so she can personally greet every student who arrives by car. 'Every day I connect with every child who gets dropped off, which is the majority of kids. We often just have a little chat, because we don't get to do those things in the classroom so much.'

She understood, however, that it was going to take more than friendly good mornings, Friday happy news stories and lunchtime meditations to help students feel better about coming back to school after lockdown.

'It was such an extended period, and there was a real disconnect. Our kids and our staff did a really good job with remote learning, but it wasn't the same. We were doing lots of things weekly for wellbeing, like discos and trivia via Zoom, but we just knew that the community would need a way to reconnect,' she explains. 'The sustained absence was causing anxiety with our kids, and we were hearing from the parents that they were anxious, too.'

Making the situation even more complex was the fact that some students *had* still been coming to school every day during the lockdowns. They were the children of frontline workers, including doctors and nurses; their parents still had to go to work, so learning from home wasn't an option. The result was a strange sort of divide between the students at home and the students on site – but the days at school weren't normal for the kids in the classroom either.

'We had a core group of about twenty kids at school every day, but for those kids everything was different.

We could be a bit free range. We took away the formal timekeeping and didn't really have bells,' Cathy says. 'A lot of the time we'd be doing our work out in the yard. We wanted to make sure those children didn't feel like they were being punished by being at school, so we were trying to replicate as much as possible what the kids at home were doing. For those kids that had been here for four or five months without other students, to then have two hundred children coming back was difficult.'

There was staff morale to consider, too. Teachers had to hit the ground running when school went online. Then, when they were finally able to return to the classroom, they not only took on the new role of unofficial counsellor to anxious students, they were also constantly scrambling to cover staff shortages that arose when their colleagues contracted COVID-19.

'Staff have never worked harder than they have in the last two years, and the pandemic is still hitting us hard. On many days we'll have five or six teachers away with COVID and no one to cover for them,' says Cathy. 'I started to really look at ways to help wellbeing.'

She knew she would need to bring out the big guns. She had to find something special, some way to remind students and teachers alike that school was a fun, nurturing and, above all, *safe* place to be in this strange new world.

And what's more fun, nurturing and protective than a dog?

*

Dogs have been making life better for humans since time immemorial, but they have only been officially 'working' as assistance dogs in Australia for the last sixty-five years. You don't have to be a card-carrying dog lover to be familiar with guide dogs. In their role as 'eyes' for people who are blind or have low vision, they have been synonymous with the concept of dogs helping people since 1957.

But the first guide dog actually arrived in Australia seven years earlier, when Dr Arnold Cook returned to his native Western Australia from the United Kingdom after completing his studies at the London School of Economics. Dr Cook, who lost his sight to a rare disease at the age of eighteen, brought home with him a fascinating souvenir: his guide dog, Dreana, a black Labrador. He had been paired with her after she was trained at Britain's Guide Dog Association.

The pair created enormous interest upon their return to Australia, with many other West Australians with low vision or blindness eager for a guide dog of their own. The first guide dog association was formed in Perth in 1951, and by 1957 there were guide dogs associations in each state.

The first guide dog to be trained in Australia was a kelpie–border collie mix called Beau. He travelled around the country promoting guide dog awareness with his mobility partner, Elsie Mead.

Today, guide dogs are mainly Labrador retrievers and golden retrievers. Puppies are born in volunteers' homes and stay there until they're five or six weeks old. They are then transferred with Mum to the puppy kennel at the Guide Dog Centre, the charity's state-of-the-art training facility at Glossodia in Sydney's west, where they stay for another two weeks.

When the puppies are around eight weeks old they go to a volunteer puppy raiser, who looks after them for a year. Puppy raisers establish good toileting, feeding, sleeping and walking routines. They also take the pup to weekly training sessions and teach basic skills, including sitting nicely when being groomed, walking well on a lead, and good house manners.

Perhaps most importantly, puppy raisers provide regular socialisation experiences and expose their pup to a wide range of environments to prepare them to accompany their eventual handler in the community.

At around fourteen months old, prospective guide dogs return to the Guide Dog Centre for a two-week assessment process. Those that pass muster then go through an intensive five-month training program with a specialist instructor to learn the skills required to navigate communities, from busy city streets to public transport. It costs around $50,000 and takes two years to train a guide dog, which is then provided free of charge to his or her handler.

But what about those that *don't* make the grade? While all guide dog pups try their best, not all are ultimately cut out for life as fully-fledged guide dogs, for a range of reasons. Fortunately, there are several other career options for those whose aptitude lies elsewhere.

'Reclassified' guide dogs can go on to become therapy dogs for both individuals and organisations, autism assistance dogs, or companion dogs. In some states they also work as court companions, providing emotional support and affection for victims of crime who have to attend court.

And yes, some reclassified guide dogs become much-loved pets – although arguably better behaved pets than the average young pooch.

Many people don't realise that guide dogs can do other things besides supporting people with blindness or low vision. It came as something of a surprise to Cathy, who lives close to the Glossodia training centre. 'I would often see the dogs training and walking around the local area, and I noticed that some wore little bandanas that said "Therapy Dog".'

An idea began to form in Cathy's mind: could a therapy dog help make her students' return to school a happier, more comfortable experience? She began to research the possibility.

'I have a colleague who has a therapy a dog at her school. She bought the dog and trained it herself. I looked into that, but the cost was prohibitive – we're only a little school.'

Refusing to fall at the first hurdle, she picked up the phone and called Guide Dogs. Cathy didn't think for a moment that Trinity would be eligible for a Guide Dogs therapy dog, but she hoped they might be able to direct her to an organisation that could help.

Instead, to her surprise and delight, they told Cathy they would be happy to provide the school with a therapy dog. There was just one catch: demand for reclassified dogs was high, and there would be a long wait.

Cathy didn't mind – she was thrilled. In August 2021, she called her staff together and pitched the idea, which was met with enthusiasm. The next step was to find a family for their new canine colleague; though the dog would be on site during school hours, they needed a loving home in which to spend the rest of their time.

'I put it to my staff and said, "We need someone to adopt them and take them home." I had four staff who were interested and we narrowed it down to the one that was most suitable,' she explains.

That staff member was learning support officer Carly Phillips. With four children, the dog would have an endless supply of attention and affection in the Phillips family's home.

'We got word in February 2022 that our application had been successful. The Guide Dogs team came out to do a site inspection and then we just had to wait for the match-up. They had to find the best dog for our school.'

That part of the process was the speediest of all. Just a week after the visit, Cathy received a call to say the perfect pup had been found. His name was Yale, and he was a Labrador who was nearly two years old.

'He had been through the Guide Dogs training but had been reclassified because they felt he was more suited to being a therapy dog,' she says. 'He wasn't strong enough on a lead, and guide dogs also have to be able to hold their bladder for eight hours, and he couldn't quite do that. He's still very good with that – he's never had an accident inside – but he wasn't quite up to the Guide Dogs standard.'

Guide Dogs provided Yale to Trinity for no charge, but the school pays for all his associated costs, including vet bills, insurance, food and grooming.

Yale's impending arrival was extra good news for Carly. Her family's beloved pet dog, Burgess, had passed away in the period since she had been selected as Yale's chief person, so he was an extra comfort to her grieving kids.

Guide Dogs instructors ran a four-hour training session for Carly, Cathy and the other staff who would be Yale's main handlers. The only thing left to do then was share the exciting news with Trinity's students.

Shortly before the end of Term 1, the students started receiving tantalising clues.

'It went for ten days and it was things like, "I'm blonde", "I like swimming", "Food is my passion", "I'm here to help". Then we tricked everyone by saying, "I'm associated with a big American university,"' says Cathy.

Each of the puppies in Yale's litter was given a name starting with Y. His was inspired by the renowned Yale University in the US state of Connecticut.

Then, in the last week of term, students and parents met for a whole-school assembly with the promise of the big reveal.

'I said to the students, "We're getting our very own . . . dog!" You can hear on the video my voice breaking as I say it. We put up a big picture of him.'

Cathy had expected the students to be excited, but she was blown away by their ecstatic response to the news. 'The reaction was amazing. They screamed the place down!'

Suddenly the return to face-to-face learning, a prospect that had previously caused so much trepidation and worry, could not come fast enough. Fortunately, the students only had to wait out the two-week school holidays before they could meet Yale in person.

While Yale was at school on the first day of the new term, which Cathy says 'was lovely', his official introduction to the children was slow and steady. He first took some time to settle into his main location at the school, Carly's learning support classroom.

'We had him down at his base and, for the first two days, we brought small groups of kids in to see him. On the third day we did a walkthrough of every classroom where the kids didn't touch him, they just looked,' Cathy explains. 'By the Friday we were walking through the classrooms and the kids were touching him.'

Only one student had expressed any concern about Yale's enrolment at the school – a little girl who had a phobia of dogs that the school had been unaware of – but even she was transformed into a dedicated Yale fan.

'After two days she said, "Next time Yale is outside, can I touch him?" We have video of her approaching and patting him. He's very calm and calming,' says Cathy.

Parents, too, have embraced Yale.

'We haven't had one negative comment. Recently I had a meeting with a parent about an illness that their child has. I said, "Is it alright if Yale is in here?" and they said, "Absolutely."'

Within weeks, Yale was part of the furniture at Trinity. If the furniture was furry and adorable and had a constantly wagging tail, that is. Just as Cathy had hoped, his gentle, non-judgmental presence on campus has had an uplifting effect on the entire school community.

His days at school are always busy. Yale arrives with Carly and they set up for the day in her classroom. He gets to enjoy a brief bit of off-lead time – during which he 'goes crazy', says Cathy – before it's time to focus on his job.

'As soon as we put the lead on him, he knows he's at work and he calms down. His window looks out to the playground and he's a very popular attraction. Everyone comes past and says hello to him,' she says. 'Typically he'll have some small groups of kids come through and do some reading with him. He goes and visits classrooms every day. He also comes to a lot of meetings, poor Yale.'

Therapy dogs thrive in the company of the humans whose wellbeing they've been trained to support, so they want to be with their people as often as possible. Guide Dogs stipulates that the dogs it provides for therapeutic purposes should not be left alone for long periods.

That means Trinity has had to be a little bit creative about keeping Yale company when Carly has to be elsewhere.

As well as his main hangout in Carly's classroom, he has a bed in the front office and a bed in Cathy's office. When he's at Carly's home, if she can't be there herself at least one of her children is usually with Yale.

'She once left him for an hour to come to an assembly, and she said he was really cranky with her,' says Cathy.

Yale has also become an important part of Trinity's rewards system. Students can earn time with Yale or the privilege of participating in some of his care tasks when they demonstrate positive behaviour.

'I said to one little student who really struggles with emotional regulation, "If you can focus on your work and keep your hands to yourself until recess, you can have five minutes with Yale,"' Cathy says. 'He gets washed here at school once a fortnight and we let some kids go out and watch that happen. He's an incentive for those children who just need something extra.'

And he is also on hand for special school events. 'At our Mother's Day assembly we had him out in the court-yard as all the mums and grandmothers came in. He was standing there so that anyone who wanted to could come and say hello.'

He's a particularly welcome presence during exams. When students in years three and five sit the annual National Assessment Program – Literacy and Numeracy test, Yale works extra hard to ease any worries they may have.

'With NAPLAN, we had a few kids who were a little bit anxious, so we did a little walkthrough to calm the kids. During his classroom visits, Yale paused in front of those nervous kids just a little bit longer,' Cathy says. 'It was like he knew which kids to go to.'

Yale even became a television star for a day when the popular breakfast show *Sunrise* visited Trinity for a live broadcast. That segment led to the story of 'Yale the well-being wonderdog' being picked up by multiple news outlets around Australia.

(His moment in the spotlight caused consternation for Carly's youngest daughter, Abbey. 'She is so in love with Yale,' says Cathy. 'When she saw the other kids patting him on TV, she said, "I hope he knows I love him more."')

In a heart-warming twist, the Guide Dogs volunteer in whose home Yale was born saw the *Sunrise* segment. He was able to get in touch with Cathy and sent her Yale's 'baby photos'.

Yale often receives fan letters – known as Yale Mail – from students, and their drawings and paintings of him adorn classroom walls. He has an Instagram account (@yaletales_trinitykc) and was a mascot during the annual sports carnival.

When school photo time rolled around, Yale even had his own portrait taken. He is not, however, a fan of being dressed up, so his willing participation in Book Week festivities is not guaranteed.

'We just want him to be part of our staff and a part of our community. We don't have any grand plans for him, but we want to think of every way we can to integrate Yale into the school day. He'll just be a part of the normal routines that schools have. We want our students to be used to him and expect him to be here.' says Cathy. 'Research points to being in nature as an important part of grounding, and our school is very rural in its outlook. We just figured that having a wellbeing dog would be another way to help with connection and engagement. Yale isn't going to solve every problem, but he's an important part of the puzzle to help the school community reconnect.'

In addition to the training Yale received to help him become a model member of the school community, the students were also taught how to interact safely and positively with him. Yale is not allowed to approach children; instead, he sits and they come to him. They, in turn, know to stop and wait until he is sitting before they get to greet him.

Of course, like any primary schooler, Yale does have days when instructions go in one ear and out the other.

'He is a bit cheeky. That's why his box of tennis balls is kept up on my desk – he finds things,' Cathy says with a laugh. 'He's very food motivated, but we only use carrot and apple as treats because he was a bit chubby when he arrived. After recess and lunch it's hard to walk him through the playground because of all the food scents on the ground. He is a scavenger, so we have to watch that.'

The great thing is that Guide Dogs' expert staff are always on hand to help iron out any behavioural gremlins. Soon after he arrived at Trinity, Yale developed a habit of barking for attention. Cathy contacted Guide Dogs, who swiftly helped her correct the behaviour.

They also gave her some advice that is relevant for all dogs, not just those with jobs. It was a reminder that dogs need patience and compassion in strange new situations, just as people do. Yale came to Trinity to help students get to grips with 'the new normal' after lockdowns, but life as a working wellbeing dog was a new normal for him, too.

'They said, "Three days, three weeks, three months." That means three days to change any behaviour, three weeks to really get into a routine, and three months to have things running the way you would expect them to be running,' she says. 'That was a good guide for us.'

Cathy concedes that it will be difficult to ever definitely say whether Yale is a 'success' as a school wellbeing dog, though she anticipates improvements in attendance, engagement and punctuality.

It will be much harder to quantify Yale's effect on students' anxiety levels and whether they enjoy coming to school. Harder by any scientific means, anyway. If you're counting smiles, pats administered or squeals of delight, then it will be easy.

Yale is top of the class.

Macca

The pandemic hero

At first glance, March 2020 appeared set to be a month much like any other. Another summer was over, and with it another horror Australian bushfire season. The leaves began to turn and evenings became cooler as autumn announced its arrival. Students settled into the swing of the new school year, their thoughts already turning to the Easter holidays.

Country music legend Kenny Rogers passed away. The Pixar animated movie *Onward* was on top at the box office. Bill Gates quit Microsoft to focus on philanthropy.

But on 11 March, the world changed – and life as Australians knew it would never be the same again. That was the day the World Health Organization declared the spread of the COVID-19 novel coronavirus to be a pandemic.

The effect of the pandemic on mental health is hard to quantify. It's almost impossible to calculate the damage caused by months of uncertainty, enforced social isolation, the dearth of hugs and kisses, the missed family gatherings, birthday parties and funerals. Nor is it possible to put a figure on the stress and exhaustion endured by doctors, nurses and other frontline workers, who have toiled around the clock to care for the sick and dying, and have borne the brunt of public fear and frustration. It is no exaggeration to say that morale in public-facing professions – from healthcare to education to retail – has never been lower.

Judy Clover knows all too well how thoroughly the pandemic has dampened our collective capacity for joy. She has worked at St Vincent's Hospital Melbourne for sixteen years, and she thrives on the bustle and energy of an institution that has 880 beds and employs almost 9000 staff across several sites.

But in March 2020, that changed. Suddenly the administrative offices became quieter, as all non-medical staff transitioned to working from home, and yet the hospital itself became busier than ever due to the influx of COVID-19 patients.

Judy is the Manager of Volunteer Services at the hospital, managing the army of volunteers that assists with everything from staffing the information desks to visiting patients. At the start of the pandemic, they were all stood down. In what felt like the blink of an eye,

Judy went from talking to dozens of people every day to almost none.

'COVID was such a drag,' she says. 'Such a mundane period of same old, same old, same old. Nobody had any news. There was nothing but the pandemic for people to talk about and focus on.'

Fortunately, even though there were no people, there were still dogs – there have always been dogs for Judy. For many years she has been able to take her dogs – Bertie and Wal, both aged seven, and four-year-old Macca – to work at St Vincent's with her (although not all at once).

Since long before her current terrific trio entered her life, dogs have been a fixture for Judy. 'I'm fifty-three and there have only been two years in my life when I haven't had at least two dogs, so I think I qualify as a dog lover,' she says.

Even before dog-friendly workplaces were more common, Judy's four-legged friends would usually accompany her to her job. In a delightful example of the myriad ways in which dogs bring people together, she had one canine colleague that inspired an enthusiastic poet to put pen to paper back in 2004.

At that time, a recently divorced Judy had a young child, so she took a school-hours job with a heavy haulage company. She would bring her Maltese–shih tzu mix, Rambo, for company. The business's office was housed in a former retail store, with the staff clearly visible through the wide shop window – except for Rambo, who preferred to sit in the doorway.

'This man pulled up once a day in a Rolls Royce. He would always carry a big bag of coins. It turned out he owned a vending machine business, and he was coming to drop the coins he'd taken out of the vending machine into the local bank,' Judy recalls. 'He was quite fascinated by the sight of me and two other people sitting in this shop window. He would see Rambo sitting in the doorway and pat him and say, "G'day mate," and strike up a conversation.'

The man's name was Geoff Denning, and in addition to being a vending machine magnate he was a published poet. He asked Judy if he could write a ballad about Rambo, and she agreed on the condition that he give her a copy.

'It's about Rambo the security dog – how he would sit in the window and protect the girls in the office and then go home exhausted at the end of the day,' she says.

Geoff duly delivered the poem to the office and Judy treasures it to this day. The tongue-in-cheek poem reads, in part:

Now Rambo is a guard dog
He'd kill if you got near
But 'cause I drive a Roller
I knew he would not fear
If I got close beside him
And told him of his looks
For men who drive Rolls Royces
Will never look like crooks

While Rambo was the dog that won Judy's heart, and she has three pint-sized dogs now, she isn't necessarily loyal to small breeds. The canine loves of her life have also included a 48-kilogram German shepherd called Ruby and an uncharacteristically large whippet called Bomber, who was was 'so goofy'.

But in recent years it has indeed been little dogs that have shared her life. At the same time as she had Bomber, Judy also had an Australian silky terrier called Rex. She decided she needed a third dog, so along came Bertie, an adorable mix of Maltese, shih tzu and poodle.

Sadly, Bomber passed away by the time Bertie actually joined the family, and tragically fourteen-year-old Rex also passed away with cancer not long after welcoming his new brother into the fold. All too suddenly, Bertie was on his own.

'Wal was the next acquisition, about six months after Bertie, because I wanted Bertie to have a mate. He gets called Walter when he's in trouble and "where's Wally?" when I'm calling for him,' says Judy.

Wal's precise breed make-up is something of a mystery, but Judy suspects he's either a Tibetan spaniel or a Sheltie mix.

Bertie and Wal were a dynamic duo for four years before Judy decided, in 2018, that a third member of the pack was once again required. She set her heart on a Yorkshire terrier after becoming smitten with a Yorkie called Harley, who belongs to a close friend.

'I thought, *I wouldn't mind a little Yorkie myself.* I got Macca from a breeder in November that year – he was an anniversary present from my husband – and found out later that he's Harley's half-brother, though he's much smaller,' she says. 'I often say we called him Macca because he's the size of a McDonald's Quarter Pounder.'

In truth, it was Judy's husband, Brett, who gave Macca his name. Bertie was named after Judy's beloved grandfather, but Brett had been the one who named Wal. He has a very specific strategy for selecting the perfect canine moniker. 'He just thinks the dogs need blokey names. Especially Wal, because he's very, very pretty – Brett thought he was too pretty, so he got named Wal.'

Introducing a new dog to a household that already has a pooch in residence is a delicate affair. It's even more important to get it right when the household has not one but *two* dogs calling the shots, especially ones so closely bonded as Bertie and Wal. Judy wanted to make sure Macca's addition to the family went smoothly, so she took two weeks off work to help the other two get used to the idea. Privately, however, she didn't think it would take anywhere near that long.

She was mistaken.

'I arrogantly thought, *This will only take a couple of days and then I can have a few days of fun and rest.* But the introductions did *not* go well,' she says. 'Wal got so aggressive towards Macca that I thought he was going to eat him. I spent the better part of a fortnight sitting on the kitchen floor, introducing them separately and then putting them all together for fifteen minutes at a time. Then I'd give them a break and do it again an hour later.'

It was an exhausting and frustrating process, but Judy was determined that all three boys would get along. Her gentle persistence finally paid off – but it took ten days for all that small-dog chest beating to settle down.

'I think Wal and Bertie got the message that I wasn't going to give up. They'd have to accept this new addition. Eventually they were okay,' she says. 'Now there's the occasional spat, but I think that's because Macca teases them. He'll run up with a toy or a piece of food and get in their faces.'

It was extra important to Judy that the three dogs learn to co-exist in relative harmony because they would need to be on their best behaviour for the new roles she had in mind for them. St Vincent's Hospital Melbourne has an in-house pet therapy program, and she wanted her dogs to be a part of it. Judy had seen what an enormously positive impact the presence of dogs in the hospital has on both patient and staff wellbeing.

'I've managed the pet therapy program and volunteers for as long as I've been in this role, but I hadn't had much hands-on involvement,' she explains. 'My overwhelming first impression was that it changed the mood on the wards – and not just for the patients. In any clinical area, the stress permeates through the staff. The presence of a dog just seems to cut through that tension. That was the thing that struck me the most: there is a benefit for every-body, not just the patients.'

Judy felt sure that her too-cute-for-words trio would only enhance those benefits. She was already taking at least one dog to work most days anyway – why not give them something lovely to do while they were there? If they could help bring smiles to people's faces and reduce stress levels, that could only be a good thing.

A few months later, when the world turned upside down, Judy discovered just how right she was; when the pandemic first hit, none of the volunteers were able to attend the hospital, so Judy's dogs were the only ones supporting patients.

The dogs in the pet therapy team at St Vincent's Hospital Melbourne are an eclectic bunch.

There are about a dozen therapy teams volunteering at the hospital, not counting Judy's dogs, each comprising a dog and their owner. They range in size from Italian grey-hounds and pugs to a Bernese mountain dog and a pair of golden retrievers.

No special training or specific certifications are needed, but each prospective therapy pooch must pass the hospi-tal's own assessment process. That's because in a varied and busy setting like St Vincent's, a dog's unique tempera-ment and relationship with their human are just as important as anything else.

'We like to see that the handler can control their dog, and that the dog is not a jumper or a biter. For example, if someone had a dog that was very young and it was in the stage where it was mouthing, it might cause skin tears in elderly people. But so long as a dog has solid obedience and a generally good temperament, there's no special testing,' Judy explains. 'What we really look for is the bond between the handler and the dog. It's no good if you have a handler that's totally besotted and saying, "My baby can do no wrong." We have to have people that are respectful of the environment of the hospital.'

Signing Bertie, Wal and Macca up to the therapy dog program had been a no-brainer for Judy. With her close-up view of the difference the dogs could make in the lives of staff and patients, she knew her charming little lads would brighten the day of anyone they met.

She didn't really need an excuse, but participating in pet therapy also gave Judy a perfect reason to bring her dogs to work with her.

'I've always been inclined to take my dogs to work in whatever job I was in, but in previous roles I was sort of inventing reasons for them to keep coming in with me. I didn't have to think twice about them becoming pet therapy dogs in this role, because there was already a built-in vehicle for me to do it,' says Judy.

Bertie and Wal had been the first cabs off the pet therapy rank. Bertie was the most regular 'therapist', coming to work with Judy at St Vincent's Fitzroy campus three days a week. Wal came too, but less often, as he sheds copious amounts of fur and had to stay mainly on the floor, which is not ideal for spending time with bed-bound patients.

When the COVID-19 pandemic took hold, however, it was Macca's time to shine. As the smallest member of Judy's pack, he was eminently portable. His size meant he was easy to lift onto patients' beds and laps. An added bonus was that Yorkshire terriers hardly shed at all, so Macca wouldn't create extra laundry.

'Macca is sweet – that's the word I would use to describe him. If you sit him on your lap and give him a pat and then you stop patting him, he's one of those dogs that will nudge your hand as if to say, *Give me a bit more of that.*'

A day on therapy dog duty is a busy one for Macca. He and Judy arrive at the hospital around 7.30 a.m., with Macca making the commute in his special doggy car seat. Now that they're allowed at the hospital again, volunteers begin arriving from nine o'clock and Macca likes to greet everyone before starting his own rounds in the wards with either Judy or her colleague Kate Bellamy.

He will comfort, cuddle and entertain patients and staff until lunchtime, when he goes for a walk with Kate and snaffles any tidbits he can from Judy's and Kate's lunches. Then he has a well-earned rest on his bed in Judy's office until it's time to go home. 'About four o'clock we head home and Macca has his dinner with Wal and Bertie. He's pretty tired after that, so the rest of the night he'll be asleep on the couch.'

Until 2019, therapy dog teams were only permitted to enter St Vincent's sub-acute departments – that is, the units where no surgery is performed. That includes palliative care, aged care and mental health. After that, the rules were relaxed to allow pet therapy to be trialled in a couple of the surgical units, including neurosurgery. It proved to be a boon during the pandemic, when so many more people desperately needed the comfort and support only dogs can provide.

And it was here that Macca really came into his own. Neurosurgery patients have often suffered severe injuries or are receiving treatment for debilitating illnesses. In both cases, many have limited mobility and significant communication difficulties.

'In the neurosurgery unit, many people are in bed or a wheelchair. We've had some great breakthroughs. There was a person who had suffered a brain event and had not spoken since. They said their first words to Macca during his visit,' says Judy. 'There was another person who'd had a stroke and had very limited use – close to no use – of one of their arms. Macca was on their bed and they moved that arm to pat him. It's amazing.'

Not having a medical background means that Judy sometimes misses these moments as they happen – but they always hit home later on. 'Sometimes I can be there and see it happen, but I don't understand the significance of it because I'm a layperson. Then someone will explain it to me and I just think, *Wow*.'

Macca's main purpose as a therapy dog is simply to provide comfort to patients and staff who may be feeling anxious or stressed – a fairly common state of existence during a pandemic, especially in hospitals. But Macca has also proved to be an effortless icebreaker, helping people who may be feeling unwell and isolated to foster new connections.

'One of the things I love is that he brings conversation and joy. Not so long ago I took Macca into a room where there were four male patients. When we went in there it was silent – they were all in their beds or chairs, staring out the window,' Judy recalls. 'I put Macca on a bed and started talking to one man, then the man opposite asked a question about Macca and joined the conversation. By the time we left, all four gentlemen were talking to one another about dogs they'd had and the dogs they have now. There was a real conversation going on and the mood in the room was uplifting and jovial. To be able to take them away from their illness and get them engaged with something that is not health related does have a great healing effect.'

She suspects that Macca's own health battles may also help patients feel a connection with him. At just six months old Macca had major hip surgery, and in early 2022 he started having seizures. He was diagnosed with epilepsy and is being closely monitored by his vet to determine whether he will require medication in the future.

Macca's gentle presence has also had an incredible effect on staff wellbeing. He is especially fond of neuro-surgery nurse-unit manager Kathryn Connor. 'Kathryn is a great advocate for pet therapy on the neurosurgery ward,' sayd Judy. 'Macca adores her. If I let go of his lead he'll go straight up the ward, turn right and go to her office.'

In late 2021, Judy decided to enter Macca in the inau-gural OZ Top Dog Awards; Kathryn wrote the submission on his behalf. Created by recruitment agency People2People and sponsored by pet supplies store PETstock, the awards are 'a feel-good competition to celebrate our furry best friends and shed some light on the positive impacts they have on our lives and mental health'.

Macca's entry detailed his critical role as a hospital mood booster and included an adorable photo of him wearing that ubiquitous pandemic fashion item, a face mask.

'We took that photo long before we knew about the competition. We were horsing around in the office one day and I said to Kate, "Put a mask on Macca." When we decided to put him in for the competition I knew we had to use that picture,' says Judy. 'I think that's what swung it for him. That's why Macca captured everyone's imagination.'

Whether it was just the cute photo, or his magical ability to connect with and lift the spirits of everyone he meets, Macca won his category. He was named Australia's Top Dog with a Job, an accolade that 'celebrates a top dog that makes a positive difference in our society for the work they do to improve human lives on a day-to-day basis'.

More than 500 dogs and their owners from around the country logged in to the live video presentation that saw Macca crowned – organisers claim it was the world's largest Zoom canine awards ceremony.

Macca was already a treasured member of the St Vincent's team, but being publicly honoured as a pandemic hero was a real cause for celebration throughout the hospital, with posters announcing the news plastering many walls. He was also featured in Melbourne's *Herald Sun* newspaper – the article included a photo with his favourite staff member, Kathryn Connor – and on Channel Ten news.

And then he went a little bit viral, with news of his win being reported as far away as India and the US.

'When his trophy arrived, we went on a bit of a tour around the hospital. It was a bit of fun in a time of great drudgery,' Judy says. 'I think Macca will remain a star, simply because everybody knows him now. We got into the lift the other day with somebody who had seen his poster on the wall and said, "Wow, that's the dog on the wall!" A nurse who's spent the last sixteen years working at the hospital recently said to me, "Oh, you're Macca's mum!"'

Throughout the peak of the pandemic, Macca was the dog that most often came to work with Judy. As life slowly returns to something approaching normal, however, she says Bertie and Wal will likely visit more frequently, too. As volunteer activities are reinstated and the hospital becomes a hive of activity once again, it seems only fair that all three dogs should experience the love that flows their way.

Further global catastrophes notwithstanding, Judy plans to continue bringing her canine colleagues to work with her for as long as she can.

'I'm guessing I'm going to retire when I'm about sixty, so that will be when Macca retires too. Then he'll be spending lots of quality time at home with us,' she says.

She can't see herself walking away from St Vincent's entirely, however – she suspects she might switch from managing the volunteers to being one herself.

Until then, Judy doesn't mind being eclipsed by Macca's star power, because what it represents is so important. Macca makes a difference. He brings joy to people who are struggling to find it. He eases worries and calms fears. He makes exhausted, burnt-out staff members look forward to coming to work every day.

And he does all of it simply by being himself.

Acknowledgements

This is the seventh book I've written about awe-inspiring and inspirational dogs, and though telling their incredible stories is never anything less than a privilege and a joy, I've got to be honest: it's been the toughest one yet.

It wasn't because of the subject matter – all the stories in this book are uplifting and life affirming, because that's what dogs are. If you cried while reading, I hope they were happy tears. No, writing this book has been a struggle because nothing makes you more aware of just how amazing dogs are than when your own amazing dogs are no longer with you.

If you have read any of my previous collections of stories about brilliant pooches, or if you follow me on social media, you'll know that for many years I've loved to write and post about my own sweet dogs, Tex and Delilah the Nova Scotia Duck Tolling Retrievers.

Aloof, inscrutable Tex (aka @thedogthatworries on Instagram) was known for his loooooong list of medical problems, and the fact that he took each one in his stride and never let his challenging health dampen his spirit. Happy-go-lucky Delilah, on the other hand, was renowned as Tex's 'silly sister', shamelessly adoring him despite his wholesale indifference towards her.

Well, I'm devastated to have to say that both Tex and Delilah have crossed the Rainbow Bridge since my last book was published. In fact, they passed away just ten weeks apart: Tex in December 2021 at the age of 14, and Delilah, just 11, in February 2022. Losing them at any time was always going to be heartbreaking, but having to say goodbye to them so close together was nothing short of devastating.

Nearly a year later, I'm not ashamed to say I am still grieving deeply for my 'best boyfriend' and my sweet 'Poss-Poss'. I miss them so, so much. The happy memories more than outweigh the sad, but I know I will never truly get over them – and to be honest, I wouldn't want to. They helped to make me into the person I am today, and they certainly inspired my career. I wouldn't change a single moment I had with them.

So first and foremost, I want to acknowledge anyone who has ever lost an adored animal companion. I see you, and I know how hard it is. Thank you for loving your four-legged friend as fiercely as you did, and continuing to do so. Please don't try to hide or trivialise your grief.

Feel all your feelings and ignore anyone who tries to belittle your loss. There is no such thing as 'just a pet'.

Thank you, too, to the people in my life who understood my sadness and did beautiful things to support me and my family. I received messages, cards and flowers from all over Australia. My favourite artist, Jane Canfield, even sent me a stunning portrait of Tex. I can never explain how much these kindnesses have meant to me.

With that in mind, a special thanks to my neurotic border collie–kelpie cross, Coco, and the newest addition to the Greaves fur family, Ferdy the flat-coated retriever, for making me smile even when I'm sad. Yes, I am aware that dogs cannot read. No, I do not care.

Thank you to all the dog owners who shared their stories with me for this book. It's been such a privilege to get to know you and your pooches, and all hail Zoom for allowing me to make silly faces at them in real time.

As ever, all the thanks under the sun to my stellar editors at Penguin Random House, Johannes Jakob and Ali Urquhart. Jojo, you have shown me more patience, generosity and understanding on this book than I had any right to expect and I am eternally grateful to you. Truly, you are the best.

My gratitude also to the marketing and publicity gurus at PRH, and the team at Penguin Audio. You are just the absolute loveliest people in all of publishing and nobody can change my mind.

to the inventors of anti-anxiety and ADHD ...on, without which I could not function, let alone ...books. If you can't make your own serotonin and ...amine, store-bought is fine!

Thanks to Karlie for being my best friend for thirty years. I've thanked you for existing in every one of my books and I'm not about to stop now.

And last but most, thank you to my family, especially my husband, Mark, and our kiddos, Miss S and Miss L. I love you more than dogs.

Almost.

More Information

BASIL
Canberra Pack Walks: facebook.com/
groups/196741044415357

BILLY
RSPCA South Australia: www.rspcasa.org.au

BRUNO
Whiskey's Wish: whiskeyswish.org.au

BUDDY
Animal Justice Party: animaljusticeparty.org

DJ
Northern Rivers Community Housing Program:
facebook.com/groups/514980876775910/

FRANKIE

Instagram: @bennyctw
YouTube: Walk2Recovery
Facebook: facebook.com/100076144024146

GROVER

Instagram: @grovermcbane
Sydney Dogs and Cats Home: sydneydogsandcatshome.org

KIMMY

Casterton Kelpie Association: castertonkelpieassociation.com.au

LEXI

Instagram: @camzschechphotography
Facebook: facebook.com/CamZschechPhotography

MACCA

St Vincent's Hospital Melbourne: svhm.org.au/support-us/
volunteers/become-a-volunteer

SALLY

Facebook: facebook.com/seniordogsbrisbane

YALE

Instagram: @yaletales_trinitykc
Trinity Catholic Primary School:
trinitykempscreek.catholic.edu.au
Guide Dogs: guidedogs.com.au

Discover a
new favourite